D0057592

# A Gentle Path

## *through the*

# Twelve Steps

### The Classic Guide for All People
### in the Process of Recovery

• UPDATED AND EXPANDED •

**Patrick Carnes, Ph.D.**

Hazelden
Publishing

Hazelden Publishing
Center City, Minnesota 55012
hazelden.org/bookstore

© 1993, 2012 by Patrick J. Carnes, Ph.D.
All rights reserved. Updated and expanded edition published 2012.
First edition previously published by CompCare Publishers 1993.
First published by Hazelden Foundation 1994.
Printed in the United States of America.

No part of this publication may be reproduced, stored in a retrieval system, or transmitted in any form or by any means—electronic, mechanical, photocopying, recording, scanning, or otherwise—without the express written permission of the publisher. Failure to comply with these terms may expose you to legal action and damages for copyright infringement.

*Library of Congress Cataloging-in-Publication Data*
Carnes, Patrick, 1944-
    A gentle path through the twelve steps : the classic guide for all people in the process of recovery / Patrick J. Carnes.
        p. cm.
    Summary: "The twelve steps tap into the essential human process of change and will be regarded as one of the intellectual and spiritual landmarks in human history. – Patrick Carnes
    It was out of his reverence and respect for the wisdom and therapeutic value of the Twelve Steps that Carnes wrote *A Gentle Path through the Twelve Steps,* now a recovery classic and self-help staple for anyone looking for guidance for life's hardest challenges. Hundreds of thousands of people have found in this book a personal portal to the wisdom of the Twelve Steps. With updated and expanded concepts and a focus on the spiritual principles that lead to lifelong growth and fulfillment, Carnes' new edition invites a fresh generation of readers to the healing and rewarding experience of Twelve Step recovery"— Provided by publisher.
    ISBN 978-1-59285-843-9 (pbk.)
    1. Twelve-step programs. 2. Compulsive behavior. 3. Alcoholics—Rehabilitation. 4. Drug addicts—Rehabilitation. I. Title.
BF632.C366 2012
616.86'06—dc23
                                                                2012006914

*Editor's note*
This publication is not intended as a substitute for the advice of health care professionals.
    Alcoholics Anonymous, AA, and the Big Book are registered trademarks of Alcoholics Anonymous World Services, Inc.
    The Twelve Steps and Twelve Traditions are reprinted and adapted with permission of Alcoholics Anonymous World Services, Inc. Permission to reprint and adapt this material does not mean that AA has reviewed or approved the content of this publication, nor that AA agrees with the views expressed herein. AA is a program of recovery from alcoholism only. Use of the Twelve Steps and Twelve Traditions in connection with programs and activities which are patterned after AA, but which address other problems, does not imply otherwise.

20 19 18 17 16    4 5 6 7 8

*Cover design by David Spohn*
*Interior design and typesetting by Kinne Design*

# Contents

# Introduction to the Updated and Expanded Edition

FOR NEARLY SEVENTY-FIVE years, the Twelve Steps have served as an extraordinary recipe for recovery. Since they were first published in the book *Alcoholics Anonymous* in 1939, they have had a profound impact far beyond the world of alcoholism, helping tens of millions of people with addictions of all types.

The Twelve Steps have been so useful and translatable because they tap into the essential human process of change and make that process more explicit, more understandable, and more sustainable. I believe that, a century from now, the Twelve Steps will be regarded as one of history's great intellectual and spiritual landmarks—one that marked our emergence into a diverse, global society.

The central premise of this book—that addiction manifests in many forms, extending far beyond drugs and alcohol—seems self-evident to contemporary readers. We now know that sex, food, money, work, relationships, shopping, gambling, gaming, and many other aspects of life can all devolve into compulsive behavior, which is the essential component of addiction. We also know that the Twelve Steps can help people with any (or any combination) of these compulsions to recover.

Today we also know that having a combination of addictions is far more common than having only one. Eighty-seven percent of people with addictions have two or more. As one Twelve Step joke notes, if some addicts went to all the meetings they qualified for, they'd do nothing else with their lives.

Twenty-five years ago our awareness was much narrower. In 1987, when the first edition of this book was proposed to publishers, many folks objected heatedly to putting alcoholics and drug addicts—or any two groups of people with different addictions— together in the same room. Many professionals saw alcoholics as very different (and slightly more refined) than drug addicts. Most other forms of addiction were given no credence at all. When I went on Phil Donahue's show to talk about sex addiction, the topic was widely perceived as a joke. Back then, looking at Twelve Step life as a whole—across addictions and fellowships—was considered a radically new, groundbreaking approach. It threatened many professionals and frightened most publishers, who also believed firmly that people wouldn't buy workbooks.

Eventually I found a publisher (not the current publisher) who would take the risk of publishing *A Gentle Path through the Twelve Steps*—but only if I would also create a set of six audio tapes. The rationale was that the tapes would do well enough to jump-start sales of the book—or, failing that, to at least offset the publisher's probable financial loss on the book.

Today, twenty-five years later, *A Gentle Path through the Twelve Steps* has sold over 350,000 copies worldwide and has become one of its current publisher's top-selling books. As for the audio tapes, they did not sell well and have been unavailable for many years. I'm not even sure where my own tapes are.

One of the hallmarks of *A Gentle Path through the Twelve Steps* has been that anybody can use it. It works for all kinds of addicts; it works for coaddicts; it doesn't matter what fellowship you are in.* Each edition of the book provides a concrete, structured way to implement what the authors of *Alcoholics Anonymous* discovered and described in the 1930s. It gives readers a focused path for integrating

---

* The words *coaddict* and *codependent* are identical. Both refer to someone who has developed an unhealthy (and usually compulsive) relationship pattern as a result of being close to someone with an addiction. *Coaddiction, codependence,* and *codependency* have identical meanings as well.

the Twelve Steps into their lives in a practical, doable way. With each new edition, my goal has been to make that path clearer, more helpful, and more profound.

Today we know so much more about the science, psychology, and sociology of addiction than we did when the first edition of *A Gentle Path* appeared in the early 1990s. We know, for example, that addictions not only commonly exist together, but interact with and trigger each other. We know that the role of family members in recovery is deeply important, and improves addicts' rates of recovery. When family members—parents, kids, and partners—commit to recovery themselves, the probability of success increases dramatically for everyone.

Perhaps most importantly, we now know immeasurably more about how the brain changes than we did even a decade ago. For a full century, the biggest obstacle to creating effective mental health treatments was that we had no way to look closely at the organ we were treating. Now, through a variety of scanning techniques, we can view the brain's activities in some detail. This has not merely deepened, but revolutionized our understanding of how recovery works. Indeed, these imaging techniques have verified and strengthened every part of the Twelve Step process. We now know that the basic neurology of recovery involves literally regrowing our brains, creating new and healthier ways of thinking, perceiving, and acting by building new neural pathways.

These new understandings have been integrated throughout this updated edition. In addition, you'll find a nontechnical, reader-friendly overview of the science behind the Twelve Steps in the prologue, "The Neuroscience of Recovery." This edition offers some new, expanded versions of many exercises and discussions. It also provides new sections on congruence in recovery and different types of recovery (partial, convenient, and inconvenient). Its appendices provide a greatly expanded list of readings, a complete listing of the many Big Books, and contact information for the forty-plus Twelve Step fellowships.

From their beginnings, the Twelve Steps have been a recipe for regrowing our brains, creating sanity, and supporting recovery. They are a proven method anyone can use—but there's more than one way to use the philosophy. In recovery we need to work whatever program we're in—but we also need the flexibility to let the process evolve into something different from what we expected. One wonderful way to support this flexibility is to learn from other Twelve Step programs. Each program offers its own unique insights and wisdom that can benefit everyone in recovery.

Today there are already some "all-addiction" meetings scattered here and there. In these meetings, people from all fellowships join together to help each other live according to the Twelve Steps. I believe that some day, perhaps not too long from now, people all over the world with addictions of every type will have access to these all-addiction meetings.

The Twelve Steps form a recipe, but following this recipe is not always easy or comfortable. Pain and hard work are inevitable on the path to serenity. Recovery is difficult because it demands that we reclaim integrity and do things we initially would rather not do. The rewards are not so visible when we begin each new leg of our journey. That's why it's so important to be kind to ourselves along the way.

From my own work as a therapist, I know how hard it is for people to be patient and kind to themselves. Each person's recovery follows its own course and timeline. The process does not have to be done fast or perfectly. Acceptance and surrender are how we become open to healing. I know a group that used *A Gentle Path through the Twelve Steps* for eleven months to get to the Fourth Step. This book aims to help you ease your way through a difficult journey.

As with the first two editions of *A Gentle Path through the Twelve Steps*, the improvements and expansions in this updated edition reflect the contributions of many hands and minds. Fellowship members, colleagues, and members of my staff all offered valuable suggestions and guidance. My thanks to them all.

— Patrick J. Carnes

# Introduction to the First Edition

THIS WORKBOOK WAS designed to help people with different types of addictions, including alcoholics, gamblers, compulsive over-eaters, and sex addicts, as well as their coaddicted loved ones. Many books exist to help recovering people through the Twelve Steps; some of them even address multiple addictions. This workbook, however, provides a unique set of structured forms and exercises to help you as a recovering person integrate the Twelve Steps into your life.

Addiction by definition possesses a driven quality. Some recovering people try to work the Twelve Steps in the same compulsive manner with which they approach their lives. The spirit of the Twelve Steps is gentleness. The path is a gentle way. Like water wearing down hard rock, consistency and time become allies in creating new channels for one's life.

I hope that the workbook becomes for you a living document that records the basic elements of your story and your recovery. A workbook well used will be filled out completely, frayed at the edges, and have margins crowded with notes. Then, like the Velveteen Rabbit that came alive with use, your living document can bring vitality to your program. It can be a way for you to think through issues as you share them with your Twelve Step group, sponsor, therapist, therapy group, or significant others.

Anonymity or confidentiality prevents me from identifying the many people whose suggestions have improved this book of forms. I am deeply grateful to all of you.

— P. J. C.

# The Twelve Steps of Alcoholics Anonymous

### Step One
We admitted we were powerless over alcohol—that our lives had become unmanageable.

### Step Two
Came to believe that a Power greater than ourselves could restore us to sanity.

### Step Three
Made a decision to turn our will and our lives over to the care of God
*as we understood Him.*

### Step Four
Made a searching and fearless moral inventory of ourselves.

### Step Five
Admitted to God, to ourselves, and to another human being the exact nature
of our wrongs.

### Step Six
Were entirely ready to have God remove all these defects of character.

### Step Seven
Humbly asked Him to remove our shortcomings.

### Step Eight
Made a list of all persons we had harmed, and became willing to
make amends to them all.

### Step Nine
Made direct amends to such people wherever possible, except when to do so
would injure them or others.

### Step Ten
Continued to take personal inventory and when we were wrong promptly admitted it.

### Step Eleven
Sought through prayer and meditation to improve our conscious contact
with God *as we understood Him,* praying only for knowledge of His will for us
and the power to carry that out.

### Step Twelve
Having had a spiritual awakening as the result of these steps, we tried to carry this
message to alcoholics, and to practice these principles in all our affairs.

• • •

The Twelve Steps are taken from *Alcoholics Anonymous,* 4th ed.
(New York: Alcoholics Anonymous World Services, 2001), 59-60.

# The Neuroscience of Recovery

OVER THE PAST decades, millions of addicts have embraced the Twelve Steps as an act of intuition or faith. Millions of others were drawn to the Twelve Steps through empirical observation—they knew other addicts whom the Steps had guided to recovery. Until recently, however, we had little scientific evidence to validate the effectiveness of Twelve Step programs.

This has all changed since the turn of the twenty-first century. Thanks to recent developments in neurology, radiology, and genetics, we now have a clear picture of how addiction takes hold in the human brain. We also have solid scientific evidence that working a Twelve Step program literally rewires our brains for recovery.

Today, through CT scans, MRIs, and other high-tech tools, we are able to look deep inside the brain. We can monitor the biochemistry of perception and emotion, sanity and sickness, compulsion and addiction, and healing and recovery. Following is some of what we now know.

- Addiction changes the brain, laying down neural networks that chemically encourage us to repeat harmful, compulsive behaviors.

- All addictions, even if they do not involve alcohol or other drugs, create the same effects in the same centers of the brain.

- Addictions are interactive. One addiction can trigger, replace, or heighten another through a measurable biochemical process in the brain.

- Trauma—whether physical, sexual, or emotional—changes the brain's chemistry, predisposing it to addictions and compulsions.

- Talk and self-help therapies that effectively change a person's thoughts and behaviors, such as working a Twelve Step program, can heal the brain in observable, predictable ways, guiding it through a process of physical restructuring. This process appears to build and deepen new neural pathways, which in turn create new patterns of thinking and acting.[1]

Advances in genetics have also deepened our understanding of addiction and recovery. If you are the child of an alcoholic, for example, you are nine times as likely to become an alcoholic than someone whose parents did not have an alcohol addiction.[2] We now know that one reason for this is genetic: when certain strands of dopamine in your DNA are shorter than normal, a heightened potential for addiction exists in your very cells.

Recent science has taught us, however, that the potential for healing and recovery is in your (and everyone's) very cells as well.[3]

We have also learned a great deal about how different addictions interact. For example, if you put a male rat together with lots of female rats that are ready to mate, the hyper-sexualized male will go on a mating binge. He'll quickly become a sex addict. Then, if you remove him, put him in with a dozen nonsexually aroused rats, and offer him cocaine, he'll immediately become a cocaine addict. This is because the sex addiction created a chemical change in his brain that responds identically to other addictive stimuli (such as alcohol and other drugs).[4]

In 1994, I began publishing articles on addiction interaction. Back then, much of what I wrote was hypothetical, based on empirical observations and my own experience. It wasn't until a few years later that we had the experimental data to back up my hypotheses. Today addiction interaction is solid science.

## Safety and the Brain

One of our most important recent findings is that safety is an essential prerequisite for healing the brain and creating successful recovery. Only when the brain feels safe can it optimally reconstruct itself. It needs to know that it is being understood and empathized with. [5]

Addicts and coaddicts typically have a problem feeling safe. Many were sexually, physically, or emotionally abused; others lived for years in an environment of fear, trauma, or continual stress. Such an environment causes the brain to produce powerful neuro-chemicals known as cortisol and endorphins. When creating these chemicals repeatedly over time, the brain can become addicted to them. This is why addicts and codependents are often drawn to drama, intensity, stress, and fear: they cause the brain to generate cortisol and endorphins. The sex addict visiting a prostitute, the gambling addict betting the rent money, the codependent husband trying to control his wife's drinking—these situations all create cortisol and endorphins in the brain. These chemicals then become two of the main drivers of addiction. [6]

Twelve Step groups create safety. Partly this is through belonging and empathy. If an addict or coaddict walks into a Twelve Step meeting and says, "This is what I'm feeling," every person in the room understands and empathizes.

Twelve Step groups also create safety through acceptance. The moment you introduce yourself ("Hi, I'm Lee"), you're completely accepted by everyone in the group ("Hi, Lee!").

As we return repeatedly to the safety of Twelve Step meetings we start to have access to balance and focus. We can then begin to face who we are and take responsibility for our life and our recovery.

## Writing a New Story

Each of us has an internal narrative about our life. We use this narrative as a way to see the world and explain it to ourselves. For addicts, this story typically involves fear, shame, victimization, blame, and anger. The more we retell this story to ourselves, and the more we see the world through the filter of our narrative, the deeper we dig the painful and habitual neural pathways in our brain. This keeps us locked in our addiction and in our repetitive, dangerous patterns of behavior.

Recent science has revealed that we can literally change our brain by retelling our story so that it includes new perceptions, new understandings, and new conclusions. As we rewrite our story, we rewire our brain by building new, more functional neural pathways. Over time, as we continue to retell this new story to ourselves and others, we strengthen and deepen those pathways, providing ever more support for our healing and recovery.[7]

As part of our recovery, our story changes over time. It begins with confusion and fear and pain, but as we work the Steps and have our own personal version of the spiritual awakening promised in Step Twelve, our story becomes less self-centered, less about victimization, and more about hope, empathy, and service. In the process, our brain steadily heals as well. The Twelve Steps are designed to support this ongoing retelling.

Telling our story also encourages the elemental human experience of bonding. In bonding, we open ourselves to others and build trust, attachment, empathy, and vulnerability. Neuroscience has proven that bonding isn't just a feeling. Our brains contain nerve cells called *mirror neurons* that help us put ourselves in others' shoes and respond emotionally to their experiences. Brain scans have revealed that when two people feel connected, the states of the mirror neurons in both people's brains take on the same patterns.[8] As psychiatrist Dan Siegel observes, "When we feel presence in others we feel that spaciousness of our being received by them. And when we reside in presence in ourselves, others and indeed the whole world are welcome into our being."[9]

## Healing the Holes in Our Heads

Any recovering addict knows that addictions create what psychologists call *impaired mental functioning*—often resulting in what we Twelve Steppers call *stinking thinking*. But brain imaging has taught us that it's much more than just thinking.

Brain scans of alcoholics and drug addicts reveal nonfunctional areas—the equivalent of holes—in their cortexes. The cortex is the part of the brain responsible for thinking and making conscious decisions. The brains of addicts thus are physically impaired, losing some of their ability to think logically, organize, pay attention, solve problems, learn from experience, control impulses, make intelligent judgments, or express empathy. Even when the addictive behavior ends, this brain impairment requires at least ninety days of sobriety to heal.[10]

Addiction creates the equivalent of holes in other parts of the brain as well. This typically results in more serious dysfunction, such as severe moodiness, increased negative thinking, decreased motivation, sleep problems, appetite problems, over- or underactive sex drive, memory problems, oversensitivity, aggression, extreme fear, extreme worry, extreme anxiety, panic attacks, obsessive thinking, and paranoia. With time, careful attention, and support, however, these brain impairments can usually be healed as well.[11]

## The Inner Observer

Recent science has taught us something even more important about the power of the Twelve Steps: the value of an inner observer.

Many of the Steps ask us to create lists—an initial personal inventory in Step Four, a list of all the people we had harmed in Step Eight, a continuing inventory in Step Ten. Even Step One requires us to make a mental list of all the ways in which we are powerless over our addiction. The process of creating each list forces us to reflect on who we are, what we have done, what we need to do, and over what and whom we are powerless.

This process creates a fundamental change in our brain. We are no longer limited to just acting and reacting. We become capable of reflecting on our own thoughts, impulses, emotions, beliefs, decisions, and actions. We create an independent inner observer that monitors and recognizes what's going on in our brain. This gives us the ability to step back and look at ourselves in much the same way that we look at others.

Our inner observer can alert us when we're headed for trouble, when we're stuck in stinking thinking, or when we need to ask for help. Psychiatrist Dan Siegel describes this as "perceiv[ing] inward—using what we've called our 'sixth sense,' so that we come to sense what we ourselves are feeling…"[12]

The work of the inner observer goes by a variety of names. It is often called *mindfulness* by meditators, and sometimes called *interoception* by therapists. Across spiritual traditions, including Buddhism, Islam, Judaism, and Christianity, a key spiritual ability is to detach and observe the traffic of the brain. Clinicians and science are catching up with these ancient practices as part of "meta thinking" or cognitive behavioral practice.

Yet, cultivating our inner observer is critical to regrowing a healthy brain. The founders of Alcoholics Anonymous understood this intuitively, even though they didn't have access to the science behind it. As a result, all the tools for creating an inner observer are embedded throughout the Twelve Steps.

### The People in Neuroscience

The important work done by neurologists, geneticists, psychologists, and psychiatrists on the brain offer us two other important insights.

First, *science is not our enemy*. It's true that, in the early decades of recovery groups, scientific knowledge about addiction and recovery lagged far behind the practical wisdom of the Twelve Steps. Much of what doctors and scientists believed back then about recovery turned out to be false. In the 1990s, however, science began to catch up, verifying one aspect of the Twelve Steps after another. Recent discoveries have also provided us with tools and insights that can make Twelve Step work even more effective. Some of these tools and insights are employed in this book.

Second, *therapists are not our enemy.* As with medicine and science, there was a time when psychologists and social workers knew considerably less about recovery than someone who had worked the Twelve Steps for a few years. But that was decades ago. Today, a good therapist can be one of our greatest allies in our recovery. In fact, I encourage most recovering addicts to work with a therapist who has a deep commitment to the Twelve Steps and an appreciation for the spirituality of recovery.

This workbook draws from the best work of these professionals and from the insights of a great many of my compatriots in recovery, as they've processed *Alcoholics Anonymous,* also called the Big Book, and its variations in different Twelve Step groups. My deep gratitude goes out to all of you.

· · ·

# Working the Program

ALTHOUGH NEW MEMBERS of Twelve Step programs often hear about "working the program," just what that means is often unclear. Each fellowship has its own definition. A bulimic, worried about bingeing, gets one response; an alcoholic, who wants a drink, gets a different one. Even in the same kind of fellowship (such as AA or OA), groups vary according to members' ages, experiences, and backgrounds. But some common elements exist that transcend the various fellowships.

Going to Twelve Step meetings is the basic building block of recovery. Just about any meeting will help, although since meetings can differ in terms of format and group chemistry, everyone should attend several meetings to find the ones that meet their recovery needs. Usually, a recovering person tries to attend one or two meetings a week, every week. Becoming involved with the life of those meetings provides a solid foundation for recovery. Making a Step presentation in the meetings or taking on a group leadership position, such as treasurer or group representative, are good ways for new members to become involved in the process. The time will come when any established meeting that is grounded in the Twelve Traditions (see Appendix A) can restore the serenity that goes with belonging to a supportive fellowship, but for beginners, as well as experienced members, having a primary group or two anchors them in a program.

Much of working a program, however, goes on outside a meeting. Most recovering people learn about the program from applying program principles to their real-life problems. Members of the group become consultants and teachers as a new member talks about the challenges of early recovery. Those relationships often last a long time. And even if they change, a recovering person learns how to get help from several sources and not to face things alone. Twelve Step fellowships assist people with dependency problems in getting support and effective problem solving.

Most groups also have a social life outside the meetings. Before or after meetings, people meet for coffee or food. Sometimes favorite restaurants become gathering spots. Some groups have regular breakfasts or lunches where people gather as sort of a second group meeting for extra support. Some groups have retreats together to intensify work on the program. While these are not part of the meeting, they can be essential to program life. To regard them as an option for which one does not have time is to miss out on an important part of developing a program for oneself: building a support network.

One major obstacle you may need to overcome as a new member is a reluctance to use the telephone. To feel comfortable only when talking about serious issues face-to-face limits your ability to use your consultants. Addicted people are not good at asking for help in general, and they will resist using the phone even at the most critical times. Thus, they stay in their isolation. Using the phone can become a habit. At first it serves as a crisis hotline. As recovery progresses, it becomes a tool for maintaining and deepening intimacy. Some program veterans hold on to their phone phobias and still put together successful recoveries. They are rare, however. Many groups urge newcomers to get a phone list and make practice calls from the start. More recently, members are using e-mail and social networks to share and get support, although it's important to use these public sites with caution to preserve anonymity and privacy.

A key figure in developing a program is your sponsor. The Twelve Steps in many ways are a demanding discipline. At whatever stage of recovery, early as well as advanced, new challenges emerge constantly in applying the Steps. Recovering people select a sponsor (sometimes two) to serve as a principal guide and witness. In early recovery, contact with a sponsor is often daily—and at times hourly. The sponsor does not have to be much more expert than you but it is recommended that he or she has been clean and sober for at least two years if possible. Your sponsor is simply someone who:

- Agrees to be your sponsor
- Knows your whole story
- Holds you accountable for how you work your program
- Keeps the focus on how the Steps apply to your life
- Remains honest with you
- Offers you support

Sometimes sponsorship evolves into friendship, but the sponsor's chief goal is to help you understand your story. Sponsors also enhance their own recoveries by helping you.

Twelve Step fellowships exist to help people stop self-destructive behavior over which they are powerless. Central to stopping the behavior is defining sobriety. Sometimes that is difficult to do. What is a slip for a codependent or a compulsive eater? Does sobriety mean just abstinence from alcohol, or is other behavior to be avoided as well? Most recovering people find that their understanding of sobriety evolves over time—and that it goes beyond just stopping self-destructive behavior. It also means embracing new behaviors. Later in this workbook you will have a chance to examine your definition of sobriety. At the outset, however, you will need to talk with your sponsor and your group about what youwill and will not do. You may be powerless over your addiction, but you are responsible for your recovery.

Many people find initiating a recovery program extremely difficult. In earlier times, the only solution when things got rough was to attend more meetings. Fortunately, professional therapists and treatment facilities now support the recovery process for the many forms of addictive illness. They have become extended partners to the fellowship. When you feel discouraged, read the "Big Book" of Alcoholics

Anonymous—the original fellowship—especially Chapters Five and Six. Composed in the days when professional support was unavailable and even hostile to Twelve Step groups, it serves as inspiration to all who wish to transform their lives.

The Twelve Steps form a process that promotes two qualities in its membership: honesty and spirituality. Starting with the first admission of powerlessness, the Steps demand a high level of accountability to oneself and others. Only one way exists to maintain that level of integrity: a committed spirituality. The fellowship becomes a community that supports this process. The program, however, is not abstract, but very concrete. You work your program whenever you:

- Make a call for support
- Do a daily meditation of the program
- Admit your powerlessness
- Be honest about your mistakes and shortcomings
- Have a spiritual awareness
- Support another program person
- Work actively on a Step
- Work for balance in your life
- Focus on today
- Take responsibility for your choices, feelings, and actions
- Do something to mend harm you caused
- Attend a meeting
- Give a meeting
- Maintain a defined sobriety

Addicts and coaddicts live in the extremes. No middle ground exists. You, as an addict, are like a light switch that is either totally on or totally off. Life, however, requires a rheostat, a switch mechanism in which there are various degrees of middle ground. Mental health involves a disciplined balance that relies on self-limits and boundaries.

Nowhere is that more evident than in the two core issues that all addicts (including coaddicts) face: intimacy and dependency.

The most obvious extreme is dependency on a mood-altering drug or experience (like sex, gambling, or eating) to cope with life. The chemical or experience becomes the trusted source of nurturing or a way to avoid pain or anxiety. All else is sacrificed or compromised. Workaholism, compulsive spending, high-risk experiences (skydiving or racing) simply fill out the range of options to lose oneself.

In the grip of addiction or obsessive behavior, life becomes chaotic and crisis-filled. Addicts and coaddicts live in excess and on the edge. Because they do not complete things, they have much unfinished business. They lack boundaries, so they often do not use good judgment. Others see them as irresponsible and lacking in common sense.

The opposite excessive extreme is grounded in over-control. Sexual obsession, for example, can be expressed as either sexual addiction or compulsive abstinence. Many adult children of alcoholics who become compulsive nondrinkers are as obsessed with alcohol as their alcoholic parent(s). An anorexic and a compulsive overeater are both obsessed with food. Over-control may be reflected in behaviors such as compulsive dieting, hoarding food or money, extreme religiosity, phobic responses, panic attacks, and procrastination.

For those with a strong need to control people, events, or their emotions, life becomes rigid, empty, and sterile. Risks are to be avoided at all costs. The fear of beginning new projects or experimenting with new behaviors is sustained by harsh judgmental attitudes and perfectionism. Living in deprivation may seem better than being out of control. But it is still an obsessive lifestyle that leads to loss of self. Recovering people can fall into a real trap if they switch from one extreme to the other and believe that the shift equals true change. The following chart shows that dynamic.

| Out of Control | Overcontrol |
| :---: | :---: |
| Alcoholism | Compulsive nondrinking |
| Sex addiction | Compulsive nonsexuality |
| Compulsive eating | Anorexia |
| Compulsive gambling | Extreme religiosity |
| High-risk experiences | Phobic responses |
| Workaholism | Procrastination |
| Compulsive spending | Compulsive saving |

| Life Becomes | Life Becomes |
| :---: | :---: |
| Chaotic | Rigid |
| Risk-filled ("living on the edge") | Risk avoidant |
| Crisis-filled | Empty |
| Unfinished | Stuck at the beginning |
| Deprived of common sense | Filled with judgments |
| Irresponsible | Hung up on perfection |
| Excessive | Deprived; impoverished |

When some of these obsessive behaviors mix, life becomes even more complex. Consider this couple: He is a sex addict and an alcoholic, and she is a compulsive overeater. She attempts to control his addiction by monitoring the websites he visits for porn and by throwing out his booze. He monitors her eating and criticizes her weight. They are both codependent. Each is obsessed with what the other is doing, each believing that he or she has the power to change the other. As his sex addiction becomes more out of control (although he believes he can control it), she becomes more nonsexual, acting as if she has the power to balance the equation. Even her excessive weight becomes a way for her to exert power by making her sexually unattractive. The reality is they are both powerless in some ways they have not acknowledged.

Variations on this theme plague couples and families in which addiction thrives. A person can even live in simultaneous internal extremes. For example, think of the bulimic who both binges (overeats) and purges (vomits). Only one way exists for people to fight living in such addictive extremes: to admit to the reality of their powerlessness.

To accomplish that task, another issue needs to be faced: intimacy. Addicts and coaddicts seek closeness, nurturing, and love. In many ways addiction derives its compelling force because of a failure of intimacy. Addictive (again including coaddictive) obsession replaces human bonding and caring.

With no emotional rheostat, you can live an isolated, lonely existence in which you build walls around yourself, deny your own needs, and share nothing of yourself. Or, you flip to an emotionally enmeshed existence in which you are so over-involved you feel trapped and smothered. You concentrate on meeting the needs of another person and take responsibility for that person's behavior. No boundaries exist and consequently no privacy exists. Again, a pattern of living in the extremes emerges.

| Isolated | Enmeshed |
|---|---|
| Deprivation | Making others' needs the priority |
| Loneliness | Smothering |
| Lack of sharing | Lack of privacy |
| Alienation from others | Feeling responsible for others |
| Rigid boundaries | No boundaries |

Add out of control with isolated—that's one extreme—and you get off center; add overcontrol with enmeshed and you get off center in another way.

## Addiction/Coaddiction: Extreme Living

Out of Control                             Overcontrolled

Isolated                                 Enmeshed

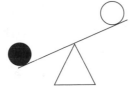 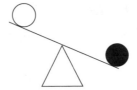

Extreme living is part of the addict's response to past or present trauma. It typically includes black-and-white thinking (dividing the world into our supporters and our enemies) and all-or-none responses (never telling our neighbor that her cat repeatedly digs up our garden, then suddenly calling the police about it).

## Recovery: Centered Living

Balance, Focus, Responsibility for Self

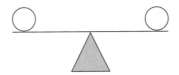

The Twelve Steps offer you a path out of extreme living. Three themes remain constant throughout the Twelve Step process: balance, focus, and a responsibility for self.

**Balance:** to avoid either–or extremes.

**Focus:** to live in the present—a day at a time—not in the future or the past.

**Responsibility for self:** to live within your own human limits.

With these three themes as a basis for living your life, recovery becomes possible.

---

◆ **My Recovery Themes** ◆

Balance

Focus

Responsibility for self

---

Before thoroughly pursuing your path, you need to secure guides to support you and help you find your way. Usually this starts with your sponsor. A sponsor is a person who works with you to help you understand the program you undertake. Other members of your Twelve Step group, or, if you are in therapy, your therapist, can also serve as guides. Record on the next page the names of your guides.

Appendix D includes a set of suggested readings to supplement the work you are doing and the guidance offered to you. A thoughtful approach on your part will enhance the workbook. Your guides will also make suggestions, especially about reading material appropriate to your program.

```
┌─────────────────────────────────────────┐
│                                           │
│          My Guides Will Be . . .          │
│                                           │
│                 Sponsor                   │
│                                           │
│    _____  │
│                                           │
│                  Others                   │
│    _____  │
│                                           │
│    _____  │
│                                           │
│    _____  │
│                                           │
│    _____  │
│                                           │
└─────────────────────────────────────────┘
```

In addition to the guides you have named above, you will receive the ongoing guidance of your Higher Power. As the Big Book observes on page 164, the essence of Twelve Step work is aligning your life with your Higher Power, however you understand Him:

> See to it that your relationship with Him is right, and great events will come to pass for you and countless others. This is the Great Fact for us. Abandon yourself to God as you understand God. Admit your faults to Him and to your fellows. Clear away the wreckage of your past. Give freely of what you find and join us. We shall be with you in the Fellowship of the Spirit, and you will surely meet some of us as you trudge the Road of Happy Destiny.

Working the Twelve Steps requires honesty, energy, and courage. At times it also requires lots of trudging through muck—your past, your emotions, and your relationships. Working the program is often a chore that requires solid, sustained effort. Put another way, we don't just experience the Twelve Steps; we *work* them. Repairing the wiring in your brain is a daily, concentrated, repetitive process. The results are real, measurable, and often remarkable. We trudge our way to sanity and serenity.

But we do not trudge alone. When the going gets difficult or painful, reach out and ask your guides—or your Higher Power—for help.

. . .

# Step One

*We admitted we were powerless over alcohol—*
*that our lives had become unmanageable.*

IN EVERY CULTURE of the world, human beings have created myths and legends to give their lives meaning and to describe the significant events and relationships that shape their experiences. In *The Hero with a Thousand Faces,* Joseph Campbell traced the origin of humanity's most universal story: the hero's journey. After studying the literature of civilizations past and present, Campbell concluded that these myths expressed important truths about the human condition. The struggles to break free from rigid, soul-stifling rules, develop a relationship with God, and express one's unique identity are universal.

The archetypes described in these myths also surface in dreams. According to Carl Jung, these archetypes represent different aspects of the human mind; our personalities divide themselves into a variety of characters who play out the inner dramas of our lives. That is why we feel a sense of recognition and identification with them. To be healthy, we need to understand the lessons they can teach us about ourselves.

One of the most important archetypes is that of the hero who overcomes adversity and becomes transformed as a result. Heroes discover, in their limitations, dramatic and unforeseen strengths. All of us have a hero within. Recovering people who have been in recovery for some time almost always marvel at the expanded awareness and renewed capabilities their suffering has brought. They have walked the ancient path of the hero.

In every sense, you are beginning the hero's journey. Most heroes, whether it be Luke Skywalker, Bilbo Baggins, or Hamlet, begin reluctantly. Forces beyond their control propel them past the busyness of their lives and into personal change and renewal. In *Star Wars IV: A New Hope*, Luke Skywalker is on a quest to destroy Darth Vader's evil empire. But Yoda, a wise teacher and spiritual guide, tells Luke of a more important struggle within. A major part of Luke's battle for peace and justice involves confronting his own shadow, or dark side. "You will face only what you bring with you," Yoda says. Luke's first teacher, Obi-Wan Kenobi, gave another warning: "Things are not what they seem. Your eyes can deceive you. Don't trust them. Reach out with your feelings."

When we're in the grip of addiction, it's easy to feel that we don't have an overarching story; we simply live in the chaos of meeting our immediate needs and trying to handle the current crisis. In Step One we realize that we *do* have a story, and that we know what it is. We also begin to tell that story. We admit we are powerless over our addiction and that our life has become unmanageable, and we accept that *this is the arc of our story up until now.*

Also embedded in Step One is the realization that this story is not hopeless or unchangeable. We are not doomed to continue to repeat it; like Luke Skywalker and every other archetypal hero, we have the opportunity to transform. Step One thus allows us to begin to see our story from a new perspective.

If you are like most addicts, you are unaware of parts of yourself, including your feelings. Without that self-knowledge, you misperceive your own reality. The First Step is designed to give you what you need to know for your journey.

The First Step requires an admission of powerlessness over living in the extremes. As part of this Step, you assemble evidence to document both powerlessness and unmanageability in your life. This is the beginning of understanding the story of your illness. Clearly specifying the history becomes essential to the unfolding of the story. The following exercises will help you in documenting your history.

**Affirmations**—Addicts and coaddicts have been negatively programmed. The experience of their illness only confirmed the damaging messages from their childhood. A list of affirmations is provided to help you reprogram. Use them daily and as you need them.

**Consequences Inventory**—You may have grown so used to life as an addict, or life with an addict, that what is normal becomes obscure. The Consequences Inventory helps to identify behaviors, attitudes, feelings, and results that indicate that life is unmanageable.

**Family Tree and Addiction**—Most addicts have other addicts and coaddicts in their families. By thinking through your family tree, some patterns may emerge that will show how some part of your powerlessness started within your family.

**Addiction History**—Addicts and coaddicts frequently have other addictions that affect their powerlessness. One example is that of the addict whose alcoholic behavior increases his sexual acting out. Another example is the codependent whose excessive weight gain from compulsive overeating increases feelings of unworthiness.

**Abuse Checklist**—Sexual, physical, and emotional abuse are common in addictive families. Children are powerless over the abuse they receive from the adults in their lives. The abuse damaged them in fundamental ways that serve as catalysts to their becoming addicted and coaddicted.

**Step One for Addicts**—Once you have documented your history in the above exercises, you'll be ready to start working and reflecting on the exercises under this heading. You'll begin to carefully document the powerlessness and unmanageability in your own life.

**Step One for Coaddicts**—In these exercises, you'll specify the type of addiction to which you are coaddicted and document your powerlessness and unmanageability.

*Note for all addicts:* A high probability exists that you are coaddicted as well. At some point you may wish to return and do a First Step on your coaddiction.

*Note for all coaddicts:* It's quite possible that you have an addiction of your own. Many coaddicts are so angry about the addiction of their partner or family member that they don't look at their own compulsive behavior. In addition, many coaddicts become compulsive about their partner's or family member's addiction. Biochemically, in the brain, their compulsion to get the addict to change is exactly the same as the compulsion to drink, do drugs, gamble, or initiate dangerous sexual encounters. If any of this rings true for you, consider doing a First Step on it.

**First Step Lessons**—Part of taking the First Step is sharing what you've learned about your story with your guides and others in the program. Remember, the answers may not come easily as you complete these exercises. When you feel stuck, get your guides to help you!

## Affirmations

One cost of addiction is loss of faith in abilities. We can learn to reprogram ourselves with positive, healthy messages.

A list of suggested affirmations follows. Each affirmation is written in the present—as if you are already accomplishing it. It may not be a reality for you today. You need to "act as if." It may be difficult, but think of it as planting a garden with possibilities that will blossom into wonderful realities.

Select from the list the affirmations that have meaning for you. Add some of your own. Tape the list of affirmations on your mirror and repeat them while you are shaving or putting on your makeup. Keep a copy in the car to repeat while commuting, or read them aloud and make a recording, then listen to them before you go to bed.

- I accept that the life I have known is over.

- I move into a new and blessed phase of my time here.

- I accept pain as my teacher, and problems as the key to a new existence for me.

- I seek guides in my life and understand that they may be different than I anticipate.

- I accept the messages surrounding me. Negativity is replaced with positive acceptance.

- I realize that I have had a hard life and that I deserve better.

- I let the Spirit melt the hardness of my heart.

- I comfort and nurture myself. As part of the surrender of my pride I will let others give to me as an act of faith in my value as a person.

- I accept my illness as part of the trauma of this culture and my family.

- I appreciate that in the chaos of the now, my instinct and beliefs may work against me. My recovering friends help me sort out healthy instincts and beliefs from unhealthy ones.

- I recognize that time is transforming my loneliness into solitude, my suffering into meaning, and relationships into intimacy.

- I do not blame or search for fault. It is not who, but how and what happened.

- I commit to reality at all costs knowing that that is where I will find ultimate serenity.

- I accept that life is difficult and that leaning into the struggle adds to my balance.

Create additional affirmations that are meaningful to you:

_____

_____

_____

_____

_____

_____

_____

## Consequences Inventory

The movie *Mask* is about a boy whose face is grossly disfigured from an illness. The story deals with the prejudice of other people and what others learn from the boy's courage. In one scene, the boy and his mother go into a typical carnival fun house and look into the distorted mirrors. Instead of reflecting his grossly misshapen face, the warped mirror reveals the image of a normal boy. He calls his mother over and they stare at what he would look like without his disease.

Addiction is like living in a fun house. The insanity and un-manageability of addiction and codependency look normal to those who can see themselves only through the distorted lens of dysfunctional behavior and its consequences. The warped mirrors of the addict or coaddict make the bizarre look normal. The following exercises are designed to break the mirrors that distort our reality.

Check each of the following that you have experienced:

### Emotional Consequences

○ 1. Attempted suicide

○ 2. Suicidal thoughts or feelings

○ 3. Homicidal thoughts or feelings

○ 4. Extreme hopelessness or despair

○ 5. Failed efforts to control the addiction or the addict

○ 6. Feeling like two people—living a public and a secret life

○ 7. Emotional instability (depression, paranoia, fear of going insane)

○ 8. Loss of touch with reality

○ 9. Loss of self-esteem

○ 10. Loss of life goals

○ 11. Acting against your own values and beliefs

○ 12. Extreme guilt and shame

○ 13. Strong feelings of isolation and loneliness

○ 14. Strong fears about your future

○ 15. Emotional exhaustion

○ 16. Other emotional consequences; specify:

_____

_____

_____

_____

## Physical Consequences

○ 1. Continued addictive behavior despite the risk to your health

○ 2. Extreme weight loss or gain

○ 3. Physical problems (e.g., ulcers, high blood pressure)

○ 4. Physical injury or abuse by others

○ 5. Involvement in potentially abusive or dangerous situations

○ 6. Vehicle accidents (e.g., automobile, motorcycle, bicycle)

○ 7. Self-abuse or injury (e.g., cutting, burning, bruising)

○ 8. Sleep disturbances (e.g., not enough sleep, too much sleep)

○ 9. Physical exhaustion

○ 10. Other physical consequences, specific to your addiction or codependency (e.g., blackouts, venereal disease, AIDS, bleeding from the throat or nose, vulnerability to disease)

_____

_____

_____

_____

**Spiritual Consequences**

○ 1. Spiritual emptiness

○ 2. Feeling disconnected from yourself and the world

○ 3. Feeling abandoned by God or Higher Power

○ 4. Anger at your Higher Power or God

○ 5. Loss of faith in anything spiritual

○ 6. Other spiritual consequences (specify)

_____

_____

_____

_____

**Family and Partnership Consequences**

○  1. Risk of losing a partner or spouse

○  2. Loss of a partner or spouse

○  3. Increase in marital or relationship problems

○  4. Risk to the well-being of your family

○  5. Loss of your family's or partner's respect

○  6. Increase in problems with your children

○  7. Loss of your family of origin

○  8. Other family or partnership consequences (specify)

_____

_____

_____

_____

**Career and Educational Consequences**

○  1. Decrease in productivity at work

○  2. Demotion at work

○  3. Loss of co-workers' respect

○  4. Loss of the opportunity to work in the career of your choice

○  5. Drop in grades in school

○  6. Loss of educational opportunities

○  7. Loss of business

○  8. Forced to change careers

○  9. Decrease in work capability (underemployed)

○ 10. Loss of job

○ 11. Other career or educational consequences (specify)

_____

_____

_____

_____

_____

**Other Consequences**

○ 1. Loss of important friendships

○ 2. Loss of interest in hobbies or activities

○ 3. Having few friends who don't participate in your addiction or your partner's addiction

○ 4. Financial problems

○ 5. Illegal activities (arrests or near-arrests)

○ 6. Court or legal involvement

○ 7. Lawsuits

○ 8. Prison or workhouse

○ 9. Stealing or embezzling to support behavior

○ 10. Other consequences; specify:

_____

_____

_____

_____

## Family Tree and Addiction

Most addicts and coaddicts come from families in which addiction or compulsive behavior was present. We learned to cope with addictive or codependent behavior by denying our feelings, wants, and needs. To help understand your powerlessness over the sources of your shame, diagram your family of origin back three generations. After entering each person's name, record any compulsive or addictive characteristics on the line below the person's name. If you are unsure, but you have a good guess about a person, simply write in the information and circle it.

In families, addictions and compulsive behavior often get passed down through dysfunctional rules, relationships, and systems. That isn't the whole story, however. Science has demonstrated quite clearly that a genetic component exists as well. The son or daughter of an alcoholic is nine times as likely to become an alcoholic as the child of someone who is not an addict. (*Important: this is a predisposition, not a certainty. No one is ever doomed to addiction because of his or her genes. Still, it can be very helpful to see the full picture of how and where addictions, compulsions, and mental illnesses have manifested in your extended family.*)

### Compulsive or Addictive Characteristics

1. alcoholic
2. compulsive gambler
3. anorexic/bulimic
4. compulsive overeater
5. sex addict
6. victim of child abuse
7. perpetrator of child abuse
8. person with a mental health problem
9. person with some other compulsive or addictive behavior such as overeating, overworking, compulsive spending, or extreme religiosity (please label)
10. coaddict

Family Tree and Addiction Chart:
# Father's Side

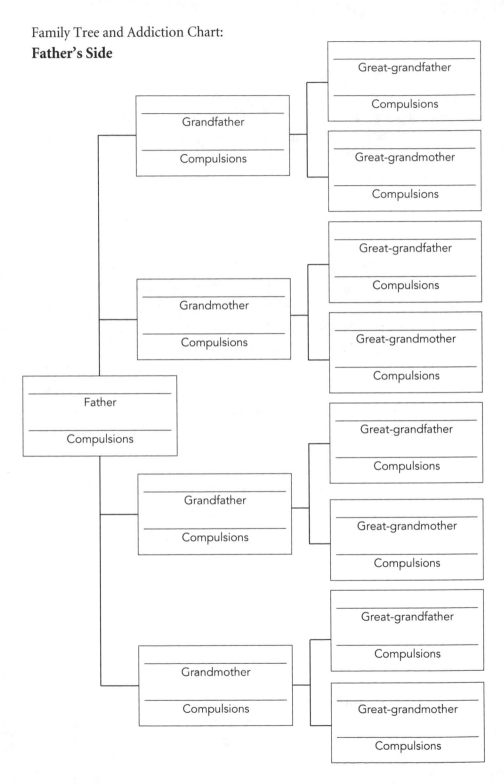

Family Tree and Addiction Chart:
**Mother's Side**

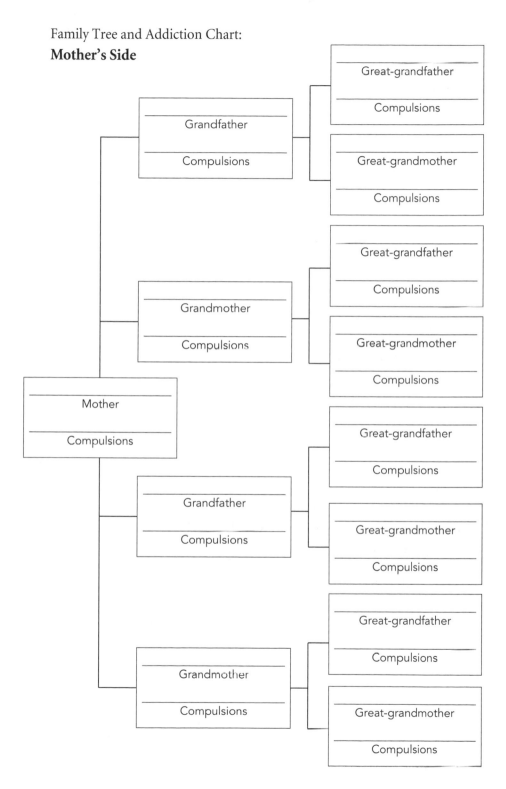

Now list any other relatives (brothers, sisters, uncles, aunts, or cousins) who fit one of the ten categories.

*Example:* Fred Smith, uncle, alcoholic, sex addict

1. _____

2. _____

3. _____

4. _____

5. _____

6. _____

7. _____

8. _____

9. _____

10. _____

Are there patterns of addiction in your family? Given the role of addiction in your family, what reflections do you now have about your own powerlessness? Can you see ways in which your addictive behavior was learned, or ways in which your behavior was a form of coping with an unhealthy family environment?

Record your reflections here:

_____

_____

_____

_____

_____

## Addiction History

Addictions and obsessions migrate. Witness the alcoholic who gets sober and then starts acting out sexually. His sexual behavior, which was already out of control, escalates dramatically to fill the obsessive void created when he stopped drinking. Our addictions and obsessions can also support one another. The compulsive gambler/sex addict who goes to Las Vegas for a multiple binge is a good example. Because addictions are "cunning and baffling" (as the Big Book notes), the type of addiction may shift from one extreme to another; for example, the compulsive overeater may become anorexic. Addictions and compulsions may become part of the family system. Consider the alcoholic whose codependent obsession with his wife's compulsive eating is an excuse for him to drink.

As part of the First Step, it helps to chronicle how various addictions or self-abusive behaviors have affected one another. Review the following categories of addictive or unstoppable behaviors. Simply write examples of how other out-of-control behaviors affected the development of your addiction or coaddiction during each age category. The notes can be short and descriptive.

*Example:* Compulsively masturbating at age 6 in order to sleep—was worse when Dad was drunk and violent—using sex to deal with my codependent fear.

*Another example:* My weight was heaviest at age 29 when I was trying to control my spouse's addiction.

| Behavior | Age 0–10 | Age 11–18 | Age 19–25 | Age 26–40 | Age 41+ |
|----------|----------|-----------|-----------|-----------|---------|
| Eating   |          |           |           |           |         |

| Behavior | Age 0–10 | Age 11–18 | Age 19–25 | Age 26–40 | Age 41+ |
|---|---|---|---|---|---|
| Using alcohol | | | | | |

| Behavior | Age 0–10 | Age 11–18 | Age 19–25 | Age 26–40 | Age 41+ |
|----------|----------|-----------|-----------|-----------|---------|
| Engaging in sex | | | | | |

| Behavior | Age 0–10 | Age 11–18 | Age 19–25 | Age 26–40 | Age 41+ |
|---|---|---|---|---|---|
| Gambling | | | | | |

| Behavior | Age 0–10 | Age 11–18 | Age 19–25 | Age 26–40 | Age 41+ |
|----------|----------|-----------|-----------|-----------|---------|
| Coaddictive behavior | | | | | |

| Behavior | Age 0–10 | Age 11–18 | Age 19–25 | Age 26–40 | Age 41+ |
|---|---|---|---|---|---|
| Other examples of compulsive behavior<br><br>*(give label— for example, shop- lifting, spending, smoking, working, risk-taking, etc.)* | | | | | |

Addictions and compulsions are often responses to abuse, trauma, extreme or long-term fear, and other extreme or long-term forms of stress. In fact, stress and fear are at the heart of all addiction.

When we grow up in an unhealthy family, the extreme or ongoing stress has a profound physical effect on our brain, causing it to create cortisol and endorphins. As we saw earlier, when these chemicals are produced repeatedly, they can themselves become addictive. We literally become stress addicts. This sets up our brain for addictions of other types.

As children, however, we may have no idea that our circumstances are unusual. We may assume that every other family is more or less like our own. As a result, not only do our brains become primed for addiction, but we don't even realize it's happening—or that there's anything unusual about the process.

This is why it is so important to fully recognize your past abuse. It has become part of your story, part of who you have become. In order to rewrite that story and grow out of it, you need to acknowledge it fully.

. . .

Now that you have completed your addiction history, think about how your addictions and codependency affected one another. How does looking at the patterns of extreme living help you in looking at your First Step?

Record your reflections here:

_____

_____

_____

_____

_____

## Abuse Checklist

Addiction studies show a high correlation between childhood emotional, physical, and sexual abuse and subsequent addiction. The following checklist and worksheet will help you assess the extent to which you were abused in your own childhood. To cope with your own abuse, you may have minimized the impact the abuse had on your life. Now is the time to recognize the abuse for what it was. Know that it was not your fault, and recognize your powerlessness over it.

Read over each of the three categories of abuse (emotional, physical, and sexual). Fill in the information in the spaces next to the items that apply to you. For each type of abuse, record the information to the best of your memory.

These are powerful memories. In thinking about these acts, be aware that an absence of feelings is a sign that you may be avoiding the work that needs to go into this Step.

| | |
|---|---|
| Age | How old were you when the abuse started? |
| Frequency | How often did it happen? Daily, two to three times a week, weekly, monthly? You may use the following scale: |

           1 = one time

           2 = seldom

           3 = periodically

           4 = often

           5 = very often

| | |
|---|---|
| Abusing person | Who abused you? Father, stepfather, mother, stepmother, adult relative, adult friend, adult neighbor, neighborhood children, professional person, brother or sister, or stranger? |

## EMOTIONAL ABUSE

| Form of Abuse | Age | Frequency | Abusing Person |
|---|---|---|---|
| *Example:* Neglect | 3 | 5 | grandparent, father |
| Neglect (i.e., significant persons are emotionally unavailable; emotional or physical care is inadequate) | | | |
| Harassment or malicious tricks | | | |
| Being screamed at or shouted at | | | |
| Unfair punishments | | | |
| Cruel or degrading tasks | | | |
| Cruel confinement (e.g., being locked in closet; excessive grounding for long periods) | | | |
| Abandonment (e.g., lack of supervision, lack of security, being left or deserted, death or divorce removing primary caregivers) | | | |

*continued*

| EMOTIONAL ABUSE (continued) | | | |
|---|---|---|---|
| Form of Abuse | Age | Frequency | Abusing Person |
| Touch deprivation | | | |
| Overly strict dress codes | | | |
| Lack of privacy | | | |
| Having to hide injuries or wounds from others | | | |
| Being forced to keep secrets | | | |
| Having to take on adult responsibilities as a child | | | |
| Having to watch beating of other family members | | | |
| Being caught in the middle of parents' fights | | | |
| Being blamed for family problems | | | |

continued

| EMOTIONAL ABUSE (continued) | | | |
| --- | --- | --- | --- |
| Form of Abuse | Age | Frequency | Abusing Person |
| Other forms of emotional abuse | | | |
| | | | |
| | | | |
| | | | |

## PHYSICAL ABUSE

| Form of Abuse | Age | Frequency | Abusing Person |
|---|---|---|---|
| *Example:* Shoving | 8, 18-30 | 5 | Mother, stepfather, spouse |
| Kicking | | | |
| Shoving | | | |
| Slapping or hitting | | | |
| Scratches or bruises | | | |
| Burns | | | |
| Cuts or wounds | | | |
| Broken bones or fractures | | | |
| Damage to internal organs | | | |
| Permanent injury | | | |
| Beatings or whippings | | | |

*continued*

## PHYSICAL ABUSE (continued)

| Form of Abuse | Age | Frequency | Abusing Person |
|---|---|---|---|
| Inadequate medical attention | | | |
| Pulling and grabbing of hair, ears, etc. | | | |
| Inadequate food or nutrition | | | |
| Other forms of physical abuse | | | |
| | | | |
| | | | |
| | | | |

## SEXUAL ABUSE

| Form of Abuse | Age | Frequency | Abusing Person |
|---|---|---|---|
| *Example:* Flirtatious and suggestive language | 6, 12-17 | 4 | Stranger, adult neighbor |
| Flirtatious and suggestive language | | | |
| Propositioning | | | |
| Inappropriate holding, kissing | | | |
| Sexual fondling | | | |
| Masturbation | | | |
| Oral sex | | | |
| Forced sexual activity | | | |
| Household voyeurism (inappropriate household nudity, etc.) | | | |
| Sexual hugs | | | |

*continued*

| SEXUAL ABUSE *(continued)* | | | |
|---|---|---|---|
| Form of Abuse | Age | Frequency | Abusing Person |
| Jokes about your body | | | |
| Use of sexualizing language | | | |
| Penetration with objects | | | |
| Bestiality (forced sex with animals) | | | |
| Criticism of your physical or sexual development | | | |
| Another's preoccupation with your sexual development | | | |
| Other forms of sexual abuse | | | |
| | | | |
| | | | |

A way to view trauma is to look at two factors. First is how significant the impact was. Second is how often the abuse happened. So, for example, you could have something happen just a few times, but it may have a very harmful effect on you. Similarly, something done that in itself is not that harmful but is done repeatedly may cause severe stress. Look at the diagram here to see the relationship between the frequency and severity of trauma and its impact.

**Impact of Trauma**

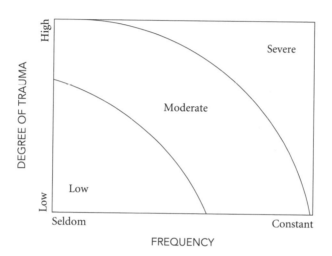

For example, if you experienced touch deprivation occasionally, you might not consider the deprivation very important. But if you were deprived constantly, you might view your situation quite differently. It is not just the quantity that is important, but how you experienced the abuse that is important.

For many of us, denying the pain and reality of what was done to us has been a source of our insanity. Accepting our powerlessness is not saying that it was okay; it is recognizing, maybe for the first time, that the abuse was not okay. Until we can accept the fear, anger, and sadness, we cannot grieve. It is our grieving that helps us to accept our powerlessness.

How has the abuse you received as a child affected you? How do you feel in reflecting on these events? What has been the impact on your addictive or coaddictive behavior? Record your answers here.

_____

_____

_____

_____

_____

_____

_____

_____

_____

_____

_____

_____

_____

_____

_____

_____

_____

# Gentleness Break

You have just completed a significant piece of work. Congratulations! Before you continue with the First Step exercise, stop and reward yourself. Choose one or more of the following activities to be gentle with yourself. If none of these appeals to you, find one of your own. If you feel compelled to keep on working, remember that you can become compulsive about the workbook, too.

Pet a warm puppy.

Play with a child.

Enjoy a long nap.

Drink a cup of tea.

Walk with a friend.

Ask for a hug—or offer one.

Do something that's fun—and not useful.

Sit by a lake or a stream.

Work in a garden.

Meditate.

Listen to your favorite music. If you like, dance to it.

Talk with a friend.

Read a novel.

Watch the sun rise or set.

Go to a park and use the swings.

Lie on the beach (or dive into the water).

Cook your favorite meal.

Skip stones across a pond.

Stick your feet in mud and wiggle your toes.

Sit with a teddy bear.

Watch your favorite movie.

Ask someone to nurture you.

# Step One for Addicts

> We admit we are powerless over
>
> _____
>
> *(insert alcohol or sex, etc.)*
>
> and that our lives have become unmanageable.

Acceptance of the First Step paves the way to recovery. As you grow to understand your own powerlessness and how unmanageable your life became when you tried to control your addiction, you begin to understand the power that addiction has had over your life. Acknowledging your powerlessness and recognizing the unmanageability in your life will help to prepare you to use the rest of the Twelve Steps.

Fill in the following chart for a clearer picture of your addiction. Either write your examples out in detail, or say a word or two that will remind you of the situation. Sharing your First Step with your group or your guides will allow them to help you in your recovery. Doing the worksheet and keeping it to yourself will not help your recovery. (See "First Step Lessons." If any aspect of addiction does not apply to you, just leave it blank.)

## Aspects of Addiction

Give three or more examples.

1. Do I obsess or fantasize about my addictive behavior?

_____

_____

_____

_____

_____

2. Do I try to control my behavior?

_____

_____

_____

_____

_____

3. Do I lie about, cover up, or minimize my behavior?

_____

_____

_____

_____

_____

4. Am I frequently trying to understand or rationalize my behavior?

_____

_____

_____

_____

_____

5. Have my behaviors affected my physical health?

_____

_____

_____

_____

_____

6. Do I feel guilty or shameful about my behaviors (or the other extreme—feel defiant or prideful about my behaviors)?

_____

_____

_____

_____

_____

7. Do I feel my emotional health has been affected by my bchaviors?

_____

_____

_____

_____

8. Have my actions affected my social life?

_____

_____

_____

_____

9. Has my school or work life been affected by my actions?

_____

_____

_____

_____

10. Have my choices affected my character, morals, or values?

_____

_____

_____

_____

11. Has my spirituality been affected by my behaviors?

_____

_____

_____

_____

12. Have my choices impacted my financial situation?

_____

_____

_____

_____

13. Have my behaviors led to contact with the police or courts?

_____

_____

_____

_____

_____

14. Has my preoccupation led to insane or strange behavior?

_____

_____

_____

_____

_____

15. Has my preoccupation led to loss of memory?

_____

_____

_____

_____

_____

16. Has my preoccupation led to destructive behavior against self or others?

_____

_____

_____

_____

_____

17. Has my preoccupation led to accidents or other dangerous situations?

_____

_____

_____

_____

_____

18. Do I keep overly or unnecessarily busy?

_____

_____

_____

_____

_____

19. Do I feel depressed a lot of the time?

_____

_____

_____

_____

_____

20. Am I able to share my feelings? If not, why not?

_____

_____

_____

_____

_____

21. Have I changed my physical image to support my addiction?

_____

_____

_____

_____

_____

22. Have I made promises to myself that I have broken?

_____

_____

_____

_____

_____

23. Have I made promises to others that I have broken?

_____

_____

_____

_____

_____

24. Have I denied that I have a problem?

_____

_____

_____

_____

_____

25. Has my addiction affected my self-esteem?

_____

_____

_____

_____

_____

26. Have I tried to relieve my pain about my behavior? How?

_____

_____

_____

_____

_____

27. Have I tried to manipulate people into supporting my addiction? How?

_____

_____

_____

_____

_____

28. Have I given up my hobbies and interests? What were these?

_____

_____

_____

_____

_____

## Powerlessness Inventory

List as many examples as you can think of that show how powerless you have been to stop your behavior. Remember, *powerless* means unable to stop the behavior despite obvious consequences. Be very explicit about types of behavior and frequencies. Start with your earliest example of being powerless, and conclude with your most recent. Generate at least thirty examples. By generating as many examples as possible, you will have added significantly to the depth of your understanding of your own powerlessness. Remember gentleness. You do not have to complete the list in one sitting. Add to the list as examples occur to you. When you finish this inventory, do not proceed until you have discussed it with one of your guides. The gentle way means you deserve support with each piece of significant work.

*Example:* Sarah said she would leave in 2008 if I slipped again, and I did it anyway.

1. _____

_____

2. _____

_____

3. _____

_____

4. _____

_____

5. _____

_____

6. _____

_____

7. _____

_____

8. _____

_____

9. _____

_____

10. _____

_____

11. _____

_____

12. _____

_____

13. _____

_____

14. _____

_____

15. _____

_____

16. _____

_____

17. _____

_____

18. _____

_____

19. _____

_____

20. _____

_____

21. _____

_____

22. _____

_____

23. _____

_____

24. _____

_____

25. _____

_____

26. _____

_____

27. _____

_____

28. _____

_____

29. _____

_____

30. _____

_____

Those examples that happened most recently will make us feel our powerlessness the most. What are the most recent examples of powerlessness? Circle five that have happened in the last ten days. Circle five that have happened in the last thirty days.

## Unmanageability Inventory

List as many examples as you can think of that show how your life has become unmanageable because of your dependency. Remember, *unmanageability* means that your addiction created chaos and damage in your life. Again, when you finish this inventory, stop and talk to your guides. You deserve support.

*Example:* Got caught stealing in 2010 to support my addiction.

1. _____

_____

2. _____

_____

3. _____

_____

4. _____

_____

5. _____

_____

6. _____

_____

7. _____

_____

8. _____

   _____

9. _____

   _____

10. _____

    _____

11. _____

    _____

12. _____

    _____

13. _____

    _____

14. _____

    _____

15. _____

    _____

16. _____

    _____

17. _____

_____

18. _____

_____

19. _____

_____

20. _____

_____

21. _____

_____

22. _____

_____

23. _____

_____

24. _____

_____

25. _____

_____

26. _____

_____

27. _____

_____

28. _____

_____

29. _____

_____

30. _____

_____

Those examples that happened most recently will make us feel our unmanageability the most. What are the most recent examples of unmanageability? Circle five that have happened in the last ten days. Circle five that have happened in the last thirty days.

# Step One for Coaddicts

> We admit we are powerless over coaddiction to
>
> _____
>
> *(insert type of addiction)*
>
> and that our lives have become unmanageable.

Acceptance of the First Step paves the way to recovery. When new to the Twelve Step program, most people find it easier to recognize the sick behavior of the addict than to recognize their own coaddictive behavior. As you grow to understand your own powerlessness and how unmanageable your life became when you tried to control the addiction, you begin to understand the power that addiction has had over your life. Acknowledging your powerlessness and recognizing your unmanageability will help prepare you to use the rest of the Twelve Steps.

Fill in the following chart for a clearer picture of your coaddiction. Either write your examples out in detail, or say a word or two that will remind you of the situation. Sharing your First Step with your group or your guides will allow them to help you in your recovery. Doing the worksheet and keeping it to yourself will not help your recovery. (See "First Step Lessons.") If any aspect of coaddiction does not apply to you, just leave it blank.

## Aspects of Coaddiction

Give three or more examples.

1. Am I obsessed with the addict's behavior?

_____

_____

_____

_____

_____

2. Do I try to control the addict's behavior?

_____

_____

_____

_____

_____

3. Do I lie about, cover up, or minimize the addict's behavior?

_____

_____

_____

_____

_____

4. Do I spend time trying to figure out the addict's behavior?

_____

_____

_____

_____

_____

5. Have I neglected my work, school, relationships, and so forth in order to spend time with the addict?

_____

_____

_____

_____

_____

6. Has my physical health been affected directly or indirectly because of the addict?

_____

_____

_____

_____

_____

7. Has my relationship with the addict had a negative impact on my emotional health?

_____

_____

_____

_____

_____

8. Has my social life been affected directly or indirectly because of the addict?

_____

_____

_____

_____

_____

9. Have there been other effects on my school or work life?

_____

_____

_____

_____

_____

10. Have I succumbed to the addict's ideas of character, morals, or values even when they were opposed to my own? (Note the effects on my character, morals, or values.)

_____

_____

_____

_____

_____

11. Has my spirituality been affected as a result of my relationship with the addict?

_____

_____

_____

_____

_____

12. Have there been financial consequences as a result of my relationship with the addict?

_____

_____

_____

_____

_____

13. Have I had contact with the police or courts?

_____

_____

_____

_____

_____

14. Has my preoccupation with the addict led to insane or strange behavior?

_____

_____

_____

_____

_____

15. Has my preoccupation with the addict led to loss of memory?

_____

_____

_____

_____

_____

16. Has my preoccupation with the addict led to destructive behavior against myself or others?

_____

_____

_____

_____

_____

17. Has my preoccupation with the addict led to accidents or other dangerous situations?

_____

_____

_____

_____

_____

18. Have I checked through the addict's mail, journals, or other personal effects?

_____

_____

_____

_____

_____

19. Do I dress to accommodate the addict's wishes?

_____

_____

_____

_____

_____

20. Do I lecture the addict for his or her problem?

_____

_____

_____

_____

_____

21. Do I punish the addict? How?

_____

_____

_____

_____

_____

22. Do I blame myself for the addict's problem?

_____

_____

_____

_____

_____

23. Do I use sex to get what I want?

_____

_____

_____

_____

_____

24. Do I make excuses to not be sexual?

_____

_____

_____

_____

_____

25. Do I attempt to persuade the addict to take care of him-
or herself?

_____

_____

_____

_____

_____

26. Am I overly responsible or irresponsible?

_____

_____

_____

_____

_____

27. Do I keep overly busy?

_____

_____

_____

_____

_____

28. Do I feel depressed a lot of the time?

_____

_____

_____

_____

_____

29. Am I able to deal with my feelings?

_____

_____

_____

_____

_____

30. Have I changed my physical image to please or displease
the addict?

_____

_____

_____

_____

_____

31. Have I believed I could or should change the addict?

 

 

 

 

32. Have I believed the addict's promises?

 

 

 

 

33. Have I denied the addiction?

 

 

 

 

34. Has the addiction affected my self-esteem?

_____

_____

_____

_____

_____

35. Do I try to relieve the addict's pain?

_____

_____

_____

_____

_____

36. Have I tried to manipulate the addict into changing?

_____

_____

_____

_____

_____

37. Have I given up my hobbies and interests?

_____

_____

_____

_____

_____

38. Has fear of rejection kept me in the relationship?

_____

_____

_____

_____

_____

39. Do I put the pieces back together after the addict creates chaos?

_____

_____

_____

_____

_____

## Coaddict's Powerlessness Inventory

List as many examples as you can think of that show how powerless you have been to stop your behavior. Remember, *powerless* means unable to stop your behavior despite obvious negative consequences. Be very explicit about types of behavior and frequencies. Start with your earliest example of being powerless and conclude with your most recent. Generate at least thirty examples. By generating as many examples as possible, you will have added significantly to the depth of your understanding of your own powerlessness. Remember gentleness. You do not have to complete the list in one sitting. Add to the list as examples occur to you. When you finish the inventory, do not proceed until you have discussed it with one of your guides. The gentle way means you deserve support with each piece of work.

*Example:* I threatened to leave home in 2011 and my spouse still did not stop drinking.

1. _____

_____

2. _____

_____

3. _____

_____

4. _____

_____

5. _____

_____

6. _____

_____

7. _____

_____

8. _____

_____

9. _____

_____

10. _____

_____

11. _____

_____

12. _____

_____

13. _____

_____

14. _____

_____

15. _____

_____

16. _____

_____

17. _____

_____

18. _____

_____

19. _____

_____

20. _____

_____

21. _____

_____

22. _____

_____

23. _____

_____

24. _____

_____

25. _____

_____

26. _____

_____

27. _____

_____

28. _____

_____

29. _____

_____

30. _____

_____

Those examples that happened most recently will make you feel your powerlessness the most. What are the most recent examples of powerlessness? Circle five that have happened for in the last ten days. Circle five that have happened in the last thirty days.

## Coaddict's Unmanageability Inventory

List as many examples as you can think of that show how your life has become unmanageable because of your codependency. Remember, *unmanageability* means that your coaddiction created chaos and damage in your life. Again, when you finish this inventory, stop and talk to your guides. You deserve support.

*Example:* In 2010, I had to get an extra job to support us because of my partner's addiction.

1. _____

_____

2. _____

_____

3. _____

_____

4. _____

_____

5. _____

_____

6. _____

_____

7. _____

_____

8. _____

_____

9. _____

_____

10. _____

_____

11. _____

_____

12. _____

_____

13. _____

_____

14. _____

_____

15. _____

_____

16. _____

_____

17. _____

_____

18. _____

_____

19. _____

_____

20. _____

_____

21. _____

_____

22. _____

_____

23. _____

_____

24. _____

_____

25. _____

_____


26. _____

_____


27. _____

_____


28. _____

_____


29. _____

_____


30. _____

_____


Those examples that happened most recently will make you feel your unmanageability the most. What are the most recent examples of unmanageability? Circle five that have happened in the last ten days. Circle five that have happened in the last thirty days.

# First Step Lessons

You have not fully taken your First Step unless you have shared it with others. One Twelve Step group has a tradition that, after ninety days in the program, a newcomer shares his or her First Step. The expectation helps remove procrastination. If you do a First Step in treatment, you may wish to do it again with your Twelve Step group. When you share your First Step, usually with a group, focus on telling about the depth and pain of your powerlessness, not necessarily your whole story. Choose incidents that are most moving to you. Get feedback and support from your guides about what to share. Remember, your goal is not to perform for others, but to help you see and accept your powerlessness. The more honest you are, the more relief you will feel.

The First Step invites you to share freely, holding little back. This is called "taking a First Step" and means a fundamental acknowledgment of the illness and a surrender to a different life. Some people go through the motions of a First Step without actually taking the Step. They avoid the Step by sharing examples of their powerlessness and unmanageability, as if they are unrelated—they are detached from the impact of their illness. Taking the Step means clearly admitting the patterns of the illness and sharing the feelings that accompany the realization that you have been out of control. Healing occurs only when the Step goes past intellectual acceptance to emotional surrender.

Following is a comparison of some of the characteristics of taking versus avoiding a Step.

| Taking a Step | Avoiding a Step |
|---|---|
| Deliberate | Hasty |
| Thoughtful | "Just reporting"; nonreflective |
| Emotionally present | Emotionally absent |
| Feelings are congruent with reality | Absence of feelings |
| Ownership of feelings; taking responsibility for behavior | Blame, denial, projection |
| Perceive that events form patterns | Perceive events as isolated |
| Acceptance | Defensiveness |
| Acknowledge impact | Deny impact |
| Surrender to illness | Attempt to minimize illness |
| See addiction as part of life | See addiction as something to be fixed |

Be aware of the tendency to become detached when telling your story. Try to remain open to both your own feelings and the feelings of those with whom you are sharing.

There are many reasons why people avoid, sometimes indefinitely, taking their First Step. Read the following items and see if any apply to you.

**Failure of courage.** To face an illness requires great courage. Some people are unable or unwilling to do it. If you find yourself thinking that you don't really need to do anything or that you can handle it by yourself, find someone in the program to support you in your fearful moments.

**Not witnessing a good First Step.** If you have never seen a First Step taken, then you have no real model of what to do. Watch someone else take the First Step, or ask your guide to talk to you about his or her First Step—how it was taken, what it meant.

**Inadequate preparation.** If you have not carefully prepared and consulted with your guides—that is, if you haven't carefully examined your own story—do not proceed. A First Step is not something you can do hastily.

**Denial of impact.** If you find yourself minimizing ("Things were not so bad") or wondering if you are making something out of nothing, it's time to go back over your story with your guides.

**Acting out.** Actively holding on to some aspect of the addiction or coaddiction, even in some very small way, will interfere with taking your First Step. Remember, you will not feel better until you completely stop your compulsive behavior.

**Holding on to a major secret.** Secrets most often involve shame, and shame will serve as a barrier to the self-acceptance necessary in taking a First Step. Share the secret with your guides or therapist before proceeding.

**Distrust of group.** Having confidence in your group is necessary in order for you to take the risks for your First Step work. If you do not feel comfortable in the group, talk to your guides about your options.

**Inadequate understanding of the Twelve Step program.** When you were brought into the program, someone probably explained how the Steps work. Each Step has a special purpose, and they were designed to be worked in the sequence in which they were written, culminating in a spiritual awakening in Step Twelve. Still, working the Steps is a lifelong program. If you are still confused about the program, seek some help before attempting your Step work.

The concept of the addictive personality shift will help you here. Addicts and coaddicts acknowledge that in their illness, it seems like there are two people inside them—the real person who tries to live up to values and cares about people, and another person whose values and relationships are sacrificed to addictive obsession. This Jekyll–Hyde experience is very common. The addict within us all is cunning and baffling. Even being able to recognize the shift from when you are your true self and when your addict has taken over is an extremely helpful tool for detaching from your addict's power.

In terms of your First Step, your addict within will work hard to sabotage your efforts at an open sharing of your illness. List below five ways your addict might try to interfere with your First Step.

*Example:* Rationalization—"When I was drinking, my boss loved my work."

1. _____

   _____

2. _____

   _____

3. _____

   _____

4. _____

   _____

5. _____

   _____

Sharing your Step work is crucial throughout the program.

**Guide Reactions**

This page is reserved for comments from your guides about your progress on your First Step. It is a place where they can write their encouragement, support, and reactions. This, too, is part of your history. Completing this page and the other guide reaction pages in this workbook is optional, not a requirement. Remember, though, that part of recovery is learning to accept support and praise, and this is a good time to begin.

Guide writes here:

_____

_____

_____

_____

_____

_____

_____

_____

_____

_____

Guide name: _____

Date: _____

# The Serenity Prayer

No better statement of our need to reestablish balance in our lives can be found than in the Serenity Prayer.

### *God, grant me the serenity . . .*

Serenity means I no longer recoil from the past, live in jeopardy because of my present behavior, or worry about the unknown future. I seek regular times to recreate myself and I avoid those times of depletion that make me vulnerable to despair and to old self-destructive patterns.

### *. . . to accept the things I cannot change, . . .*

Accepting change means that I do not cause suffering for myself by clinging to that which no longer exists. All that I can count on is that nothing will be stable—except how I respond to the transforming cycles in my life of birth, growth, and death.

### *. . . courage to change the things I can, . . .*

Giving up my attempts to control outcomes does not require that I give up my boundaries or my best efforts. It does mean my most honest appraisal of the limits of what I can do.

### *. . . and wisdom to know the difference.*

Wisdom becomes the never forgotten recognition of all those times when it seemed there was no way out, and new paths opened up like miracles in my life.

For many of us in recovery, the Serenity Prayer begins as a way to let go and process our grief about life. Over time, however, as we work the Steps and let them work on us, the Serenity Prayer becomes a way of living. The Serenity Prayer is a recipe, not a formula. It does not have hard and fast boundaries, and its applications are ever-changing. We must continually adapt it to our circumstances. In the process, it teaches us how to steadily adapt to the challenges of life.

## Reflections on the First Step

On this page, and on pages like it at the end of each chapter, you are asked to stop and summarize your feelings about the Step you have just taken. It's important for you to appreciate the ground you have already covered, as well as to consider ways to keep from losing that ground.

Now that you have taken and shared your First Step, reflect on what it means to you. Reflect also on the Serenity Prayer. What things can you do to make the philosophy contained in this prayer part of your daily life?

## The Recovering Brain

The most important element of recovery is the ability to choose.

Addiction robs much of our power of choice by hijacking our brain, over and over, until we become powerless over our addiction and our life becomes unmanageable.

But addiction does not take away every choice from us. In Step One, we choose to acknowledge our powerlessness and admit what our life has become. We accept our limitations and the realities that addiction presents to us.

This Step connects us to memories that show us how our addicted brain has seduced and hijacked us. These memories help us wake up to how cunning addiction is. We can look back and see that many of the decisions our addicted brain made were harmful ones. Only then can we begin to recognize the stinking thinking that is part of our addiction. Only then can we begin to know what wise decisions look like.

As we work Step One, we plant the seeds of discernment. Then, as we work the remaining Steps, we practice decision-making by reviewing and analyzing our past decisions to see which ones were helpful and which ones were harmful. We then create a map of our past decision making. This helps us to better understand how our addiction functions—and it helps us make better decisions in the future.

By studying human cognition through brain scans and other tools, science has discovered that eight different parts of the human brain are involved in decision making—and all eight closely interact. If even one of these eight parts is not working properly, we don't think clearly, and our ability to make decisions is impaired. Neuroscience has discovered that addictions and compulsions negatively affect all eight of these areas.[13]

For years, researchers tried to determine which of these eight areas was the most important, or which one might serve as a leverage point in treating addiction. Now, finally, we have the answer: *all eight areas are essential.* For successful recovery, we must reclaim the ability to use all eight.

## Celebrating Your Progress

Congratulations on completing your First Step, so crucial to your recovery. If this Step has left you open to shame attacks, you may want to spend a lot of time with people in the program who will help you stay on the gentle path. Suggestion: Create a celebration for yourself to mark your progress!

What are some of the gentle, healthy ways you can celebrate the new beginning you have made? What are some of the ways you can celebrate your progress as you work the program during the coming weeks and months?

_____

_____

_____

_____

_____

_____

_____

# Step Two

*Came to believe that a Power greater than
ourselves could restore us to sanity.*

# Step Three

*Made a decision to turn our will and our lives over
to the care of God* as we understood Him.

I WAS RAISED CATHOLIC. It was Christmastime, and I was in the first grade. The priest of our little country parish called my mother and asked if I could serve as an altar boy on Christmas morning. I expressed some fear because I had never done it before, nor had I been through the "altar boy training program." He told me to come early that morning and he would show me all I needed to know.

On that fateful morning I dutifully showed up early. My mother, thrilled at the prospect of my serving at Mass on Christmas morning, had invited her five sisters and their families to join us. This had now become a high-drama event. My fear was escalating. Old Father Yanny, however, was very reassuring. There were only two things I had to remember. One was when I was to move the Holy Book from one side of the altar to the other. The second was to ring a set of bells whenever he put his right hand on the altar. In those days, the bell was a signal to the congregation to kneel, sit, or stand at different points in the liturgy.

Father Yanny was getting on in years. He probably wasn't aware that he often leaned on the altar to steady himself—using his right hand. When he leaned, I rang. When I rang, the congregation moved. I had that congregation going up and down, up and down. My mother was mortified. My aunts thought it was great, and they tell the story to this day.

Whether it was right or not, the people moved when the bell rang. As an adult, I think of that experience as a metaphor about religion. For many, it often seems like a forced or meaningless motion. How many of us have become detached from a spiritual life because the ritual does not fit our lives?

I remember a patient who told this story about family week. It was Sunday morning and his spouse was attending service in the church across the road. He sat in his room, looking at that church, knowing she was inside. He was moved by her faithfulness, especially about how important their relationship was to her. With that emotion he had a flash of insight about how he had put faith in the wrong things as part of his illness. With the tears that came, he felt connected to his partner and the presence of his Higher Power. For most, the story is the same. Spiritual things happen when you admit suffering.

Ultimately, this question of meaning is a spiritual one. Steps Two and Three ask, Whom do you trust? In whom or what do you have faith? How much you trust others often parallels your trust in a Higher Power. If you have trouble accepting help from others and insist on handling things alone, chances are you will resist the help of a Higher Power in your life. Many addicts who have worked the program realize that if they refuse help after admitting that they are powerless and damaged, they will remain stuck in their insanity.

The First Step asks you to admit that you have an illness. Steps Two and Three ask you to confront the question of what gives your life meaning. Without meaning in your life, your addiction and co-addiction can grow and thrive. Without meaning, you cannot establish the priorities that help you restore the balance, focus, and self-responsibility you seek.

Six things will make these Steps easier:

**Spiritual Care Inventory**—This inventory focuses on your spiritual needs and helps identify obstacles to completing Step Two and Step Three.

**Loss-of-Reality Inventory**—This inventory helps you focus on your priorities.

**Paths to Spirituality**—The exercises in this section allow you to reflect on some spiritual moments you may have experienced but hadn't identified as spiritual.

**Spiritual Path Affirmations**—These affirmations will help replace the negative messages and ideas we learned about God with positive ones.

**One-Year-to-Live Fantasy**—This exercise in confronting your own death provides perspective on the spirituality and meaningfulness of your life.

**Letter to Your Higher Power**—This exercise offers a concrete way to express your spiritual decisions.

Remember to include your guides in this process.

## Spiritual Care Inventory

### Openness to Spirituality—A Self-Assessment

Consider the following statements and the choices to complete the sentence. Make a check mark next to the choice that best describes your usual behavior.

In a grocery store, when searching for something I cannot find,

○ I keep searching until I find it.

○ I ask for help.

When putting something together from a kit,

○ I follow directions carefully.

○ I quickly go through the instructions only when I get stuck.

○ I figure it out for myself.

When I am personally in pain and need support,

○ I talk to people immediately.

○ I wait until the crisis is over and then tell people.

○ I get through it the best way I can without help.

As you responded to these situations, did you discover a pattern of not letting yourself be helped? Often addicts and coaddicts rely solely on themselves.

As an addict or coaddict, you have relied on your obsessions to deal with pain and difficulty. You may have learned not to depend on people for help, care, and support. It is probable that you learned not to accept help based on the way your primary caregivers treated you as a child. Consider the following list of people. How did each affect your ability to receive help? Were you given support when you made a mistake? Were you shown how to do things, or were you expected to know without being taught?

Your father

_____

_____

_____

_____

_____

Your mother

_____

_____

_____

_____

_____

_____

Brothers and sisters

_____

_____

_____

_____

_____

_____

Other relatives

_____

_____

_____

_____

_____

_____

Teachers (specify)

_____

_____

_____

_____

_____

_____


Employers (specify)

_____

_____

_____

_____

_____

_____


Clergy (specify)

_____

_____

_____

_____

_____

_____

Other significant adults (specify)

_____

_____

_____

_____

_____

Review the following list of feelings and states of mind that commonly occur among people in recovery. Describe your own feelings when it becomes necessary for you to ask for help.

| | | |
|---|---|---|
| helpless | resisting | individualist |
| scared | nontrusting | detached |
| uncertain | questioning | cooperative |
| tentative | testing | nurturing |
| confused | loner | guiding |
| vulnerable | unique | assisting |
| rebellious | free | directing |
| challenging | separate | reliable |

From the list of twenty-four words above, select the six words that most aptly describe you.

Now these same twenty-four words are arranged below in terms of dependence, counterdependence, independence, and interdependence. Find the six words you selected above and circle them again. Have you circled three or more words in any one category?

| Dependence | Counterdependence | Independence | Interdependence |
|---|---|---|---|
| helpless | rebellious | loner | cooperative |
| scared | challenging | unique | nurturing |
| uncertain | resisting | free | guiding |
| tentative | nontrusting | separate | assisting |
| confused | questioning | individualist | directing |
| vulnerable | testing | detached | reliable |

The terms can be defined as follows:

- **Dependence**—We need and want help.
- **Counterdependence**—We need help but resist it.
- **Independence**—We are self-sufficient and do not need help.
- **Interdependence**—We give and get help to and from others.

**Higher Power Attitude Index**

Now that you know how you normally react when you need help from others, you may take a spiritual attitude inventory. Accepting your reality does not mean making excuses for continuing with your insanity. It means you recognize where you are and how you need to change to become responsible for yourself.

Circle six of the words below that best describe how you understand your Higher Power.

| | | |
|---|---|---|
| judgmental | loving | absent |
| strict | purposeful | disengaged |
| negative | compassionate | hoax |
| rigid | predictable | unreal |
| cruel | distant | nonexistent |
| arbitrary | indifferent | fanciful |
| caring | uncaring | imaginary |
| trustable | nonattentive | joke |

Your perceptions of a Higher Power have evolved over the years. Before you can be truly reflective about a Higher Power, you need to clarify your attitudes toward God. Four ways of viewing God exist for many of us:

- **A punishing God** who punishes our mistakes but does not reward or help.

- **An accepting God** who accepts that we fail and cares anyway.

- **A noninvolved God** who is detached and unconcerned with our lives.

- **A nonexistent God** who is not available to offer help.

From the list of twenty-four words above, you selected six words that most aptly described your perceptions of God. In the chart on the next page, these twenty-four words are arranged into four columns, each representing a different view of God: punishing, accepting, noninvolved, or nonexistent. Circle the six words you selected previously. Does any category have three or more words circled?

| Punishing | Accepting | Noninvolved | Nonexistent |
| --- | --- | --- | --- |
| judgmental | caring | distant | hoax |
| strict | trustable | indifferent | unreal |
| negative | loving | uncaring | nonexistent |
| rigid | purposeful | nonattentive | fanciful |
| cruel | compassionate | absent | imaginary |
| arbitrary | predictable | disengaged | joke |

Are there patterns in the words you selected?

_____

_____

_____

_____

_____

Are there any correlations between the adjectives that describe your Higher Power and the descriptions of how the caregivers in your life helped you?

_____

_____

_____

_____

How have your perceptions of God or your Higher Power
changed over time?

_____

_____

_____

_____

_____

_____

_____

How does your current mode of accepting help (dependent,
counterdependent, independent, and interdependent) fit with
your perception of God or your Higher Power?

_____

_____

_____

_____

_____

_____

_____

Who are the five persons who most influenced your attitudes toward God or your Higher Power?

1. _____

2. _____

3. _____

4. _____

5. _____


Do they have anything in common?

_____

_____

_____

_____

_____

_____


What obstacles does your religious background or upbringing give you for trusting in a Higher Power?

_____

_____

_____

_____

_____

_____

What strengths does your religious background or upbringing give you for trusting in a Higher Power?

_____

_____

_____

_____

_____

_____

_____

_____

Based on what you have learned about recovery so far, how do you see the "turning over" process of Step Three? What are the things that might prevent you, emotionally and intellectually, from accepting the help of a Higher Power?

_____

_____

_____

_____

_____

_____

_____

_____

In what ways do you see a Higher Power working in your life now?

1. _____
   _____

2. _____
   _____

3. _____
   _____

4. _____
   _____

5. _____
   _____

6. _____
   _____

7. _____
   _____

8. _____
   _____

9. _____
   _____

10. _____
    _____

## Loss-of-Reality Inventory

Even after recognizing the unmanageability of our lives in the First Step, many of us still do not want to use the word *insanity* to describe our own behavior and thinking. Denial and delusion come from addictive and coaddictive impaired thinking. Considering that insanity involves some loss of touch with reality, addicts and coaddicts need to regain perspective on what is real and what is not. Spirituality will continue to elude us if we persist in delusion. The following are three descriptive categories of loss of reality.

**1. No reality.** You lose your memory from a combination of factors, including obsession, overextension, exhaustion, anxiety, and intoxication. Or, you lose contact with here-and-now events because of the same combination. One recovering coaddict described her experience with loss of reality: "We were newlyweds in our first year of marriage. One night my husband was arrested for voyeurism. I functioned perfectly through that embarrassing night, and when I awoke the next day I had forgotten all about it. And I continued to have no memory of it for thirty years, until two years ago, when I started my own recovery. Now I can remember every detail, the colors, what I wore, every minute."

Reflect on your own experiences with no reality and loss of memories.

_____

_____

_____

_____

_____

_____

_____

**2. Distorting reality.** Reality is blurred because of the power the addiction has over you. Think of things you thought were true because your addict wanted them to be true. Or, think of how you have distorted reality because of faulty beliefs. (If you start with a faulty belief, such as "Women have to be seduced in order to enjoy sex," your thought processes will naturally be faulty as well. You may believe, for example, that seduction is the only way to get sexual needs met.)

Reflect on your own distortions of reality.

_____

_____

_____

_____

_____

_____

_____

_____

_____

_____

A group in Colorado developed a distorted core belief exercise called "I'm only lovable if . . ." Examples are "I'm only lovable if I'm sexual," "I'm only lovable if I'm perfect," "I'm only lovable if I don't ask for anything."

Complete your own "I'm only lovable if . . ." delusion exercise.

I'm only lovable if _____

_____

I'm only lovable if _____

_____

I'm only lovable if _____

_____

I'm only lovable if _____

_____

**3. Ignoring reality.** When you ignore reality, you fail to assess risks accurately. Or you overcome the recognition that recent experiences were disastrous by your compulsion to repeat them. An addict knows the penalties but goes ahead and does the act anyway. Risking unsafe sex, financial overextension, job loss, arrest, car accidents, loss of marriage, and legal consequences are all examples of ignoring reality.

Describe specific examples when you ignored reality and suffered immediate consequences.

_____

_____

_____

_____

_____

_____

Describe specific examples when you ignored reality, escaped any immediate consequences, and may have believed that you dodged a bullet—but then suffered consequences later on.

_____

_____

_____

_____

_____

_____

Describe specific examples when you ignored reality and appear to have escaped all consequences (at least so far).

_____

_____

_____

_____

_____

_____

Describe specific examples when you went back and forth between accepting and ignoring reality, either experiencing the two fight endlessly in your brain, or obsessing continually about the choice but not actually choosing.

_____

_____

_____

_____

_____

_____

_____

_____

### Grieving Your Losses

Now reflect on your losses of reality. When you needed help, whom did you ask? Specifically what did you ask for, and how did you make your request? When you asked your Higher Power or other people for help, was your request based on reality?

_____

_____

_____

_____

_____

_____

_____

_____

Being willing to ask for and accept help, and being able to trust that others will help you, are central to living a spiritual life.

Many addicts are unwilling or unable to ask for help because of our painful experiences growing up. We may have been shamed or punished for asking for help, or people may have simply ignored or discounted us.

If people failed to help us when we asked them for help we genuinely needed, it's no surprise that we have trouble asking for help now.

Think back to when you were young. In your family, who was it safe to ask for help, and who was it not? When people did provide help, how did they give it? How helpful were they? Did you often have to figure things out on your own?

_____

_____

_____

_____

_____

_____

_____

When you were growing up, did your family ignore some obvious realities? Were there subjects they refused to talk about? What were those topics, and why were they taboo? What did you do when you needed help with something involving a taboo topic?

_____

_____

_____

_____

_____

_____

_____

_____

When you needed help growing up, were there people outside your family whom you could ask for assistance? Who were they? How did you ask them for help? How did they usually respond? How helpful were they?

_____

_____

_____

_____

_____

_____

_____

Do you have trouble asking for help now? Do you feel there are people willing and able to help you? Do you feel your Higher Power is willing and able to help you? Do you feel you are worth helping?

_____

_____

_____

_____

# Paths to Spirituality

Across world religions and throughout the history of human experience with the Divine, we find certain universally recognized strategies to nurturing spirituality. While each person's experience is unique, these ways of approaching life maximize our availability to spiritual presence. Each of the following is a common path others have taken. We suggest you use each thought as a meditation to reflect on and journal about over the next ten days.

### Be as a Child

Children live fully in the moment. Adults are distracted by the past and concerned about the future; children live in the now. Adults focus on what is practical; children focus on what is. Every parent has had a chance to see through a child's eyes and marvel at the world adults often miss. Children are totally engaged in what is happening around them. They want to explore and understand everything, immediately, with all their senses. It is easy to be intimate with children because they are so vulnerable and open. Spirituality is about intimacy—closeness and appreciation of oneself, others, and a Higher Power.

For some of us, to be vulnerable and open was to risk exploitation. So we built defenses and coping mechanisms that split us off from our experiences. It is partly how we lost our spiritual connection. In the safety of recovery, the challenge is to reclaim our vulnerability and openness so we can be present to the world.

Reflect on what you would have to do to be more present in your life. Record your thoughts here:

_____

_____

_____

_____

_____

_____

_____

_____

_____

_____

## Connect with the Earth

Our senses are the gateway to a spiritual life. They put us in touch with the complexity, beauty, and wonder of creation. Reflect on the most peaceful and serene moments of your life. Notice that nature was somehow usually involved. Mountains, seas, sunsets, and woods create awe and tranquility. It is this peace which connects us to the larger picture of the universe.

Indigenous peoples are sustained spiritually by connection with the planet. They live with the immediacy of growing things. What they eat, they hunt or gather. They have a sense of what had to die that they might live. So they respect creation but are matter-of-fact about life and death. They do not miss the central reality of their existence. They are part of a larger ecology with intelligence and purpose. To survive means to acknowledge the larger rhythms of the planet.

Contemporary peoples tend to be removed from these life realities. They create buildings for spiritual life because they experience only the community, not the connection with nature. They are often not aware of where their food comes from, nor do they have any sense of its life—or where they fit in the food chain. They fear death and see nature as something to be overcome. Then they agonize over their existential aloneness.

For many recovering people, the beginning of a spiritual life started with some reconnection with the planet. What ways are available to you? Record them here. Pick one to do today, and others to do in the next weeks.

_____

_____

_____

_____

_____

_____

_____

_____

_____

_____

_____

_____

_____

## Develop a Beginner's Mind

When a Zen warrior or monk practices "emptying the mind," it literally means discarding preoccupations and fears and being in the moment. This means emptying the mind of all preconceived conditioned thought or prejudice—to be totally open to the moment and what it may teach. The beginner learns to appreciate the moment for what it is—a new experience. To be most responsive—whether for battle or discernment—one gives no thought to the outcomes.

Joseph Campbell and others who have studied the hero's myths in many lands notice that a similar process is central in every hero's journey. The hero comes to a point where he or she must stop worrying about what to do or how to overcome the obstacles in the way, and just do what needs to be done. Right action comes by taking the next step. But first the hero must surrender or submit to the teaching of a spiritual guide or mentor. Through this process, the hero learns the inner discernment necessary to make wise decisions. The relationship between Luke Skywalker and Yoda clearly reflects this process. Not until Luke fully sets aside his pride and surrenders does he experience the full power of The Force.

Initiation rites in primitive cultures mark an individual's passage from one state of being to a higher level. The initiate (or beginner) never knows exactly what is going to happen, but allows designated members of the community to direct the ritual process. Usually this surrender involves pain, just as it does for the hero. The initiate's suffering taps into new strengths, and new destinies emerge. The initiate is fundamentally changed.

Sadly, we lack these rites in contemporary culture. Recovering people, however, have much in common with the initiate, the hero, and the Zen master. Steps One through Three demand surrender without knowing what will happen. With surrender comes pain and transformation. Recovery is like the hero's journey or the initiate's ordeal. Once we have begun, there is no going back. With each turn in the road, we must empty our minds once again. If we are to fully experience the unfolding reality of our lives, there is no other path.

List the obstacles in your life to the "beginner's" mind.

_____

_____

_____

_____

_____

_____

_____

_____

_____

_____

## Access Your Own Wisdom

Emptying ourselves of distractions, preoccupations, and obsessions allows us to connect with who we really are. Henri Nouwen described this early stage of spiritual life as the "conversion of loneliness into solitude." It means discovering what Dietrich Bonhoeffer called "the ground of our being." It is finding the sacred within us. When we are true to ourselves, we are most spiritual. That means tuning in to our own authentic voice.

How do we do that? Think of your own life experience. Think of the times you had an intuition that something was not going to work out, but you did it anyway. And when that turned out to be a disaster, you said, "If only I had listened to myself." Carl Jung talked about a larger consciousness that we can tap into with our intuition—if we would listen. This is called _discernment_—the ability to see clearly what is, especially in those situations when we have no rules, laws, or prior experience to direct us. This is where divine guidance and trusting ourselves meet. All heroes come to this crossroads where they do not know the outcome but must act.

To cultivate discernment, keep a regular journal, develop a daily meditation routine, listen to music that makes you feel like yourself, and read what helps your insight and sense of self. If you work at it, your true voice—the one that is in harmony with the larger universe—will become clear.

There is no magic to this process—though often there is mystery in it. At times you will experience a knowing, or come to a decision, without understanding why or how you got there—but you'll know that this knowledge or decision is right.

List five times you have ignored your inner voice. For each incident, write down the consequences of not listening to it.

1. _____

_____

_____

_____

_____

2. _____

_____

_____

_____

_____

3. _____

_____

_____

_____

_____

4. _____

_____

_____

_____

_____

5. _____

_____

_____

_____

_____

Now list five times you listened to and followed your inner voice. For each incident, write down the consequences of listening to it.

1. _____

_____

_____

_____

_____

2. _____

_____

_____

_____

_____

3. _____

_____

_____

_____

_____

4. _____

_____

_____

_____

_____

5. _____

_____

_____

_____

_____

In what ways can you deepen your own discernment?

1. _____

_____

_____

_____

_____

2. _____

_____

_____

_____

_____

3. _____

_____

_____

_____

_____

4. _____

_____

_____

_____

_____

5. _____

   _____

   _____

   _____

   _____

## Care for Your Body

Loving and nurturing your body is a metaphor for every spiritual task you face and is the primary spiritual act. Jigoro Kano, the revered founder of modern judo, thought that physical discipline was a gateway to spiritual growth. Mastering the technique was the least important part. Facing your fear, emptying yourself, trusting your own voice, letting go of control, having faith in outcomes, connecting with a larger purpose, deriving meaning from the struggle—that is the primary work of the athlete. Kano also taught that physical development was a lifetime commitment—not a casual task, nor only for the young. Like the Greeks, he saw physical exercise as an essentially spiritual discipline that we must practice until we die. In the West, we tend to see fitness as an optional health concern that can be a low priority in a busy schedule. We make physical fitness into a competition and confer status symbols—Olympic gold medals or multi-million-dollar contracts—on a few gifted athletes. Occasionally, when someone refers to the runner's high or the "zen" of weightlifting, we glimpse the more profound connection between mind and body. When we separate these positive experiences from the rest of life, we split the two and add to our spiritual damage.

Here is the reality: Our body is the primary vehicle through which we experience our world. As the custodian of the organism in which we reside, we must nurture and tend to it. We must stretch and grow. Anything less splits us off from one of the central sources of awe about creation—our bodies. It is the most concrete way we have to embrace the spiritual struggle that teaches us. A contemplative life is not an inactive one. It requires the gentle but continuous flow of our energy.

List obstacles to an active physical life.

1. _____
2. _____
3. _____
4. _____
5. _____
6. _____
7. _____
8. _____
9. _____
10. _____

How many of these obstacles could be restated as obstacles to a spiritual life? (Example: not enough time.) Put a check after each one that would be true of both. Record your reflection about the commonalities.

_____
_____
_____
_____
_____
_____
_____

## Search for the Circles

The circle is a sacred symbol of connectedness. Plants, animals, and people decay and die and are replaced by new growth and the miracle of birth. Seasons recycle the earth. Everything and everyone is nestled in this larger connectedness. In central Africa, the symbol is a sacred snake configured so it consumes its own tail. Native American peoples used the sacred hoop to signify the four points of the compass. Christians have used the circle to describe life, death, and resurrection.

Theologian Paul Tillich described sin and grace from this perspective. He said that sin was about action that separated you from yourself, others, and God. Grace originated in connection with yourself, others, and God. The Navajo use the phrase "being in harmony." When we truly experience this source of belonging and connecting, we find extraordinary meaning in our lives. We can understand the words of Chief Seattle when he said, "You must teach your children that the ground beneath their feet is the ashes of their grandfathers."

Holding hands in a Twelve Step meeting and saying the Serenity Prayer is the first experience of reconnection for many recovering people. In time they grow to realize that at any time, night or day, there is a group somewhere saying that prayer. With further understanding, they realize that each person's struggle is important to all the other members of the group, and ultimately, to all the groups. The recovery process itself is a rebirth out of the ashes. And with each person who makes it, the whole is better. In fact, the entire planet is better.

In the space that follows, draw a picture of your support community, using circles. Do not use any words, just indicate connections. After completing the drawing, what do you notice?

### Find Spiritual Guides

In our obsessions, we are fiercely committed to handling things on our own. If we consult others, the temptation is to give them only part of the story or share after the crisis is over. To allow someone to see the full extent of our despair when it is happening in all of its untidy, ugly, and searing reality is a tremendous leap of faith. We resist it, since to acknowledge the wound is to experience the pain. We are not expected to do this alone. Absolutely essential to a spiritual path is allowing ourselves the gift of help.

Spiritual guides come mainly in three ways. First, we find trusted persons who can teach us from their own wounding experiences. We tell them how it is for us. Their perspective and support ease the pain. They give us concrete ways to connect with our Higher Power. Sponsors, clergy, therapists, mentors, teachers, elders—all come in this category.

Second, we seek spiritual community. We find spiritual guidance in groups of people—Twelve Step fellowships, religious communities, men's and women's groups—also committed to walking a spiritual path. We will connect with spiritual guides wherever we find that we are not alone, and there are celebrations and symbols of our progress together.

Finally, we are open to guidance from others around us every day. The answers to our struggles are surrounding us if we listen to the possibilities. An offhand comment by someone may have been exactly what we needed to hear. Watching some creature live its life can be a metaphor for what we need—if we allow for the possibility. Asking questions like *How am I like the wolf, the turtle, or the wren?* or *How does an animal greet pain, make herself comfortable, or use caution?* opens us to a deeper connection with the natural world—and ourselves. By analogy, we can meditate on the significance for our own lives.

Reflect for a moment on how you receive direction in your life. Do you seek it, using it as a way to expand your potential? Or do you resist it and see it as an intrusion? Who have been your guides so far? How well have you used them? Record your thoughts below.

_____

_____

_____

_____

_____

_____

### Accept Pain as a Teacher

All of us have suffered. For some, it is caused by the trauma of betrayal, neglect, or exploitation. Sometimes the source is a cataclysm that seems to have no purpose beyond destruction. All of us experience change. So we have the grief of that which is no more. A Buddhist definition of suffering is "clinging to that which changes." Twelve Step programs basically teach us to adopt an existential view of change and suffering. It is best summarized in the Serenity Prayer.

**God, grant me the serenity**

**to accept the things I cannot change,**

**courage to change the things I can,**

**and wisdom to know the difference.**

Viktor Frankl, in his study of survivors of the Nazi concentration camps, noticed that those who survived had a common quality: the ability to transform suffering into meaning. Spirituality is about meaning and asking questions like *Why do bad things happen?* and *Who is in charge of it all?* We tend to war against difficult issues when they surface in our lives. We talk of "my fight against cancer." Part of a spiritual path involves learning to "see my illness as a teacher."

Suffering simply is. It's not fair, right, or wrong. It simply is. However, how I respond is critical. How I take action, how I grow, and how I become a more spiritual person is the most important thing. Remember the fundamental lesson the Greeks taught in their tragedies. The hero typically suffered from a tragic flaw—*hubris*, or the sin of pride. Oedipus and the other great heroes refused to accept their human limitations and made themselves into gods. Whenever they ignored their own limitations and wounds, however, they met a tragic fate. Our wounds help us to accept our humanness and be open to the lessons provided for us.

Make a list of five painful experiences in your life. Then list some reasons why you have come to value those experiences.

1. _____
   _____
   _____

2. _____
   _____
   _____

3. _____
   _____
   _____

4. _____
   _____
   _____

5. _____

_____

Think of your struggles. What are the lessons for you now? Record your thoughts here.

_____

_____

_____

_____

_____

_____

_____

_____

_____

## Develop Spiritual Habits

Recovering people can often remember traumatic experiences in childhood that altered their lives. But it was the daily experience of living in the family which had the greatest impact. So it happens with spiritual life. Spiritual experiences occur that alter one's life. But it is the daily spiritual practices that bring spiritual depth. St. Paul told us of his conversion experience on the road to Damascus. Yet it is he who cautions that "every day we are surrendered unto death." Native Americans echo this belief when they say that the only thing one needs to do each day is pray.

Another way to view daily spirituality is to think of it as a relationship. Relationships are not sustained by dramatic encounters, but by daily efforts which over time deepen the relationship. To develop a spiritual relationship with your Higher Power takes commitment and time. Having a regular routine makes a dramatic difference. Starting is difficult. We do not see results immediately. Sponsors often suggest that we "act as if." Allow the time. Start with simple readings and meditations. Diets, exercise programs, developing new skills—all those things are difficult at first. But regular, daily work makes a difference.

One of the key discoveries is that you can make your own rituals and prayers. While many participate in spiritual communities, each person's journey is unique. So we can add our own symbols, our own patterns of meditation. We discover reflections that help us and modify them for our own use. Spirituality evolves from groping when we are in trouble, seeking to extend our internal life.

Write below your daily spiritual recipe. Describe it as if you were explaining it to someone who wanted to practice what you do. If you are not doing anything currently, describe what recipe might work for you.

_____

_____

_____

_____

_____

_____

_____

_____

## Work on Steps

Each of the Twelve Steps contributes to our spiritual life.

**Step One** confronts the paradox of our addictive and coaddictive processes. We feel powerful when, in fact, we are powerless and need help.

**Step Two** challenges our grandiosity and reminds us that we are limited human beings.

**Step Three** underlines our efforts to control when we need to take responsibility only for ourselves and leave the rest to our Higher Power.

**Step Four** takes the energy out of the shame that separates us from ourselves, others, and our Higher Power. It brings acceptance.

**Step Five** asks us to break through the paralyzing fear that prevents us from receiving forgiveness and faith.

**Step Six** attacks our perfectionism, allowing us to experience our wounds so that we might heal.

**Step Seven** asks us to give up our willfulness so that we might allow change to work in our lives and to begin grieving.

**Step Eight** asks us to exchange our pride for honesty.

**Step Nine** challenges us to stop seeking approval and to pursue integrity by making amends for harm we have caused.

**Step Ten** makes a daily prescription to set aside our defenses and admit our errors.

**Step Eleven** asks us to trade the magical thinking of escapism for the realities of a spiritual life even though they are difficult.

**Step Twelve** tells us to trade in our martyr-like victim roles and share the changes in our lives with others with similar problems.

The following chart summarizes the effects of the Steps upon addictive and coaddictive behavior.

| In our addiction we were . . . | | In our recovery we seek . . . |
|---|---|---|
| deluded | Step One | reality |
| grandiose | Step Two | a sense of limitations |
| controlling | Step Three | faith in others |
| shameful | Step Four | self-worth |
| fearful | Step Five | forgiveness |
| perfectionistic | Step Six | healing of brokenness |
| willful | Step Seven | letting go |
| prideful | Step Eight | honesty |
| approval-seeking | Step Nine | integrity |
| defensive | Step Ten | responsibility |
| escapist | Step Eleven | connectedness |
| self-suffering | Step Twelve | witnessing our path |

The Big Book of Alcoholics Anonymous tells us that if we do these things, certain promises will be fulfilled:

> We are going to know a new freedom and a new happiness. We will not regret the past nor wish to shut the door on it. We will comprehend the word serenity, and we will know peace. No matter how far down the scale we have gone, we will see how our experience can benefit others. That feeling of uselessness and self-pity will disappear. We will lose interest in selfish things and gain interest in our fellows. Self-seeking will slip away. Our whole attitude and outlook upon life will change. Fear of people and of economic insecurity will leave us. We will intuitively know how to handle situations that used to baffle us. We will suddenly realize that God is doing for us what we could not do for ourselves.

What reactions or reflections do you have about the promises for yourself? If you were to write your own version of the promises to pass on to others, what would you write? Record them here.

_____

_____

_____

_____

_____

_____

_____

_____

## Spirituality Affirmations

The following list of suggested affirmations will help you reprogram yourself for spiritual openness. Read them each day, or make a voice recording of these positive messages and listen to them before falling asleep at night. Select from the list the affirmations that have meaning for you, and add some of your own. Gradually, as you repeat these affirmations to yourself, you will begin to experience and internalize your inner truth. Affirmations are a spiritual gift you can give to yourself.

- *Each moment of my day is filled with openness and vulnerability to the world around me.*

- *I am connected to my planet. I experience the sky, the wind, the rain, and all the elements of my environment. I am aware of the cycle of life. Each day brings greater awareness of my place in this universe.*

- *With an empty mind, I take in each moment as a new experience. Each moment in recovery brings transformation.*

- *I have an inner, true voice that is in harmony with the universe. Each day I develop greater acuity and discernment in interpreting my voice's clear messages to me.*

- *My body is my primary vehicle for embracing the awe of my world. Each day I nurture and tend to it. Stretching my body brings energy, strength, and confidence to face my struggles.*

- *I am connected to the past, present, and future. What has gone before me is part of me and I will be a part of what goes on after me. I am part of the circle of my community. As we are all connected to the past, present, and future, we are all connected to each other.*

- *I am open to the spiritual guidance of others. My spiritual guides are those I love and trust, those I respect, those who have a message for me and those who offer symbols to help me on my journey.*

- *My wounds are my teachers. I am open to their lessons.*
- *I practice my spirituality daily. My spirituality is a daily extension of my internal life.*

### I Affirm the Promises for Myself

- *I know a new freedom and happiness. I embrace my past.*
- *I comprehend the word serenity and know peace.*
- *I can see how my experience can benefit others.*
- *That feeling of uselessness and self-pity has disappeared.*
- *As I lose interest in selfish things, I gain interest in my fellows.*
- *Self-seeking has slipped away.*
- *My whole attitude and outlook upon life is changing.*
- *Fear of people and economic insecurity has left.*
- *I intuitively know how to handle situations that used to baffle me.*
- *I realize that God is doing for me what I could not do for myself.*

### I Affirm the New Learnings of the Program

- *I cannot end or manage my addiction on my own.*
- *I cannot control other people's thoughts or actions of others. The more I try to control others, the more problems I create.*
- *I cannot foresee the future.*
- *My powers are limited. Often I need help from my Higher Power, from other people, or both.*
- *Uncertainty is a part of life.*

Create additional affirmations that are meaningful to you.

_____

_____

_____

_____

_____

_____

_____

_____

_____

_____

_____

_____

_____

_____

_____

_____

_____

_____

_____

## One-Year-to-Live Fantasy

Reclaiming reality starts with a clear sense of our limitations as human beings. But we live in a culture that denies these limitations. We are constantly invited to overextend ourselves—for example, to spend more than we earn, work more than we need to, or eat more than we should. We live as if there were no end. We literally deny our own mortality.

A powerful exercise that can show you your own limitations is to picture your own death. Looking at death provides vital perspectives about what gives your life meaning, what priorities you are ignoring, and who your Higher Power is.

Make a voice recording of the following fantasy, then set aside some uninterrupted time to listen to it and answer the questions provided at the end. Pause for ten to fifteen seconds where indicated before you continue. Make sure you are physically comfortable. If you do not have a recording device, you may read the fantasy, or have your guide or a close friend read it to you.

### Fantasy

*Imagine that you are in your physician's office. What does it look, smell, and feel like? Your doctor comes in and tells you that results from the tests are in. You have a terminal illness. All the other doctors consulted agree. They think you will maintain your physical ability for about a year—but at the end of the year you will die.* [pause]

*Imagine your first reactions as you walk out of the office. What do you do?* [pause] *How do you spend those first few hours and days?* [pause] *Do you tell anyone?* [pause]

*As you start to adjust to your dying, do you change your life? Stop work? Do something different?* [pause]

*Maybe you want to do something different. Perhaps you wish to travel. Where would you go? Picture yourself traveling. Whom would you bring with you? [pause] Perhaps you might want to do things you have never done before. Activities like skydiving, scuba diving, race car driving seemed too dangerous before, but now it doesn't make any difference. What have you always wanted to do but been afraid to do? [pause] Picture yourself doing this. Who is with you? [pause]*

*Almost all of us have unfinished parts of our lives: a book we are writing, a family room to finish, a family project such as getting the family album in order for the kids. What unfinished projects would be important enough to finish before you die? [pause] Imagine yourself doing them. [pause]*

*For some of us, the unfinished parts include things not said to others—like "I'm sorry" or "I love you." Picture yourself saying the things you would need to say before you die. [pause]*

*It's now about three months before you die. You can start to feel your health fail. While you can still function, you decide to try one last thing. What would that be? [pause] What would be one of the last things you would want to do before you die? [pause] Who is with you? [pause]*

*It's now a matter of weeks before you die. Where do you go to die? [pause] Your home? A family farm? A lake? The mountains? The city? [pause] How do you spend those last days? [pause] Who is with you? [pause]*

*As you think over the events of this last year of your life, what were the most significant ones for you? [pause] In fact, think of these and all the events of your life. Which stand out now as the things that made life worthwhile? [pause]*

*As you reflect on these events, be aware that you are working on this workbook. And you are very much alive. Be aware of your current surroundings. Wiggle your fingers and toes to bring yourself all the way back to the present, and become ready to move on to your next activity.*

**About the Fantasy**

Often this fantasy helps people touch their own grief about losses in their lives. If you feel sad, do not avoid the feelings. Rather, use them and let them support you in coming to terms with your losses. Sharing the fantasy and your feelings with your guides can deepen your understanding of the issues the fantasy raises. First, record the details of your fantasy in the space provided. Then answer the questions that follow.

Describe your first reactions.

_____

_____

_____

_____

_____

_____

List the changes you would make in your life.

_____

_____

_____

_____

_____

_____

_____

List the new things you would try.

_____

_____

_____

_____

_____

_____

_____

Explain the unfinished things you would want to complete.

_____

_____

_____

_____

_____

_____

_____

State the things you would need to say before you die.

_____

_____

_____

_____

_____

_____

_____

Describe what your last fling would be.

_____

_____

_____

_____

_____

_____

_____

Explain the spiritual preparation you would take.

_____

_____

_____

_____

_____

_____

Describe where and how you would spend your last days.

_____

_____

_____

_____

_____

_____

Throughout the fantasy, there were key moments involving significant persons in your life. Name those you would involve and what you might learn about your relationship priorities.

_____

_____

_____

_____

_____

_____

_____

During the fantasy, you may have found yourself doing things significantly differently from how you live now. Why would this be so? What prevents you from doing those things now?

_____

_____

_____

_____

_____

_____

_____

How do you feel about facing your own death?

_____

_____

_____

_____

_____

_____

Thinking about death provides a way to look at what is real and what is important in our lives. How have your ideas of what is important and real to you changed after experiencing this death fantasy? What can you change in your life now to reflect these new priorities?

_____

_____

_____

_____

_____

_____

# Gentleness Break

Before proceeding, take a gentleness break. You have already accomplished so much, and you need some time to care for yourself before going on. Following are some suggestions.

**Read a story to a child.**

**Rediscover the fun of doodling with colored pencils or crayons.**

**Do a crossword puzzle or Sudoku.**

**Paddle a canoe.**

**Walk by a lake or stream.**

**Smell a flower.**

**Watch some birds. Feed them if you like.**

**Sit in a church or other place of worship.**

**Invite a friend out to dinner—or invite a friend to take you out.**

**Get a massage.**

**Go for a run or jog.**

**Ride your bike (or your motorcycle, skateboard, etc.).**

**Lie on your back and look up at the sky.**

**Play your favorite game with a friend.**

**Make up a song and sing or hum it.**

**Relax in a bubble bath.**

From this point on, there will be no more scheduled gentleness breaks. It's up to you to pace yourself and to determine when to take a break and how to spend that gentle time.

### Letter to Your Higher Power

The Second and Third Steps become very concrete when you write a letter to your Higher Power. By writing this letter, you turn your belief and trust into an active process.

Here are some things you might include:

- How you "came to believe"

- What the decision to turn over your will and your life means to you (Be specific about what you are turning over.)

- How you feel about your life right now

- The aspects of recovery that have brought you relief or serenity

- The parts of recovery that are difficult, painful, or frightening for you

- How you feel about the future, including your hopes and your fears

- Your doubt or disbelief about your Higher Power

- Moments or events in your life that you know were not accidents (Be specific, and reflect on these events as important parts of your life.)

- What you are grateful for

- Requests for help (Be specific.)

People use many different names in addressing their Higher Power, but what seems to work the best is when you make it as personal as possible.

When you have written the letter, read it aloud to your guide. We need to share our spiritual experiences with others to make sense of them.

Dear _____,

_____

_____

_____

_____

_____

_____

_____

_____

_____

_____

_____

## Reflections on the Second and Third Steps

Trusting life comes from making some meaning of who we are, of what we are all about. When we confront shame, we become aware of emptiness, a spiritual hunger. Our attempts to fill this hunger with controlling, compulsive behaviors only lead to pain and remorse. Carl Jung was aware of this compulsive "filling of the void." He wrote to Bill Wilson, the cofounder of AA, saying that he thought alcoholism was the search for wholeness, for a "union with God."

— Merle A. Fossum and Marilyn J. Mason
*Facing Shame: Families in Recovery*

Reflect on the Fossum/Mason quote above and how you feel about the Second and Third Steps in your life.

_____

_____

_____

_____

_____

_____

_____

_____

_____

_____

_____

_____

_____

_____

_____

_____

_____

_____

_____

The Second and Third Steps are very personal transactions and create a special intimacy when shared with others in the program. Ask the guides who have shared in your process to record their personal reactions here.

_____

_____

_____

_____

_____

_____

_____

_____

Guides: Express the trust or faith you have in the work the owner of this workbook has done.

_____

_____

_____

_____

_____

_____

_____

Guide name: _____

Date: _____

Psychotherapist Viktor Frankl wrote eloquently about how our suffering can be transformed into meaning. Frankl observed that there are three ways of finding meaning in life: (1) giving or contributing something to the world through our work, (2) experiencing something or encountering someone, and (3) choosing a courageous attitude toward unavoidable suffering.[14]

This third source of meaning is particularly valuable for addicts, because it teaches us that suffering is not what it seems. As we work the Twelve Steps, we learn that every painful experience can become a source of meaning or wisdom.

The Second and Third Steps are fundamentally about finding what gives your life meaning and passion. This includes the meaning found in the acceptance of unavoidable suffering.

This insight mirrors what neuroscience teaches us: that our brain functions at its best when it is engaged in a healthy activity that it is passionate about or that gives it meaning.

Addicts are passionate about their addictions, of course. When we're in the throes of our addictions, drugs or alcohol or sex or gambling or codependence feel—very temporarily—like they satisfy our brain and make our life meaningful. But, like suffering, this momentary satisfaction is not what it seems. The simple truth is that addictions tear apart the brain.

The Second and Third Steps ask us to look at what *really* gives meaning to our life. Part of this involves learning how to create wisdom and resilience from painful experience, and recognizing that the struggles of recovery are worthwhile. These activities serve and satisfy the brain in ways that addiction never can.

# Step Four

*Made a searching and fearless moral inventory*
*of ourselves.*

# Step Five

*Admitted to God, to ourselves, and to another*
*human being the exact nature of our wrongs.*

WITH THE FIRST STEP you admitted your powerlessness and vulnerability. The Second and Third Steps helped you gain the support you need from your Higher Power and other people to face the reality of addiction and coaddiction in your life. With that support you can make a fearless moral inventory and use it to examine the damage your illness has caused. This thorough self-assessment will impel you to let go of much of what keeps you in your compulsive patterns. Recovery requires giving up the old ways in which you nurtured yourself by living in the extremes. In that sense, the Fourth and Fifth Steps are a grieving process. The feelings that go into the grieving process in the Fourth and Fifth Steps include discomfort, anger, fear, shame, sadness, and loneliness. Discomfort is the outer layer of feelings, anger the second layer, and so on down to the innermost feeling of loneliness.

These feelings, which are layers of your internal self, serve as a barometer of how you feel about your behavior. They can also be a structure on which you build your moral inventory.

You will find the Fourth Step inventory to be a deeply personal experience, with each layer guiding you to a deeper relationship with yourself.

Notice, however, that the innermost layer is loneliness, in which you confront the existential reality of your aloneness and estrangement. However, the program, in its wisdom, asks you in the Fifth Step to find and share with another person the work you have done on your Fourth Step. You do not need to be alone. The program builds in more support for you at each difficult turn in your path.

The person you select to hear your Fourth Step can be someone in the program, a sponsor, or a member of the clergy. In addition to being deeply personal, the Fourth and Fifth Steps are spiritual experiences.

Before starting on your Fourth Step, set a time with the person who will hear your Fifth Step. There are several reasons for doing this. First, the Fourth Step is an awesome task and easy to put off. By making an appointment, you make a commitment to get the task done. Even if you have to reset the appointment, the focus will be on getting the Step done. Second, the person who will hear your Fifth Step may have some suggestions for you to help you in your process. Finally, you will know for sure that someone will be there for you when the path becomes difficult and painful. Again, do not forget to involve your other guides in the process as well. You do the task yourself, but you do not have to be alone. Each section will generate feelings. You do not have to wait to share them. Talk about them as they stir, not after you have figured them out.

Within each layer of feelings, you will find elements of your moral inventory that are good and positive as well as negative. As you survey the wreckage caused by your illness, you may assume that a Fourth Step focuses on all the failures, mistakes, and harm done. However, to restore integrity means to claim the successes, the goodness, the courage, and the effort as well.

Sometimes, when things seem dark, it is difficult to claim the positive in your life. If it is difficult to take credit for positive things in yourself, look at it this way: In your addiction, you probably worked hard to cover the dark side of yourself and showed only the good parts to the world. You lived between the secrets, shame, exploitation, and abuse of your hidden addict and the care, responsibility, and values of the public you. You probably even felt phony about your public self, because people did not know the real you behind the image you showed to the world. When you face the addict within you in the Fourth Step, your addiction becomes your teacher about the goodness in you. Ask yourself, Was your addict strong? Enduring? Clever? Willing to risk? Resourceful? All these are qualities your addict borrowed upon to become powerful. They are equally available to you in your recovery.

Unfortunately, many people attempt a recovery by doing the opposite of what they did in their active illness. They focus only on the bad side and bury the good. The Fourth Step presents an opportunity for you to reclaim those good parts of yourself and use them for your recovery. This is a difficult challenge, to be sure, but the result is that you get to be the real you. You don't have to have an addictive, dark side draining all your power in its secrecy. And you don't have to feel phony or insincere when you own all parts of yourself. Besides, it is much easier to face your recovery secure in the knowledge of the good things you do have to draw upon. It is the more gentle way.

The Fourth Step is a demanding and even draining experience. Pace yourself. Take several gentleness breaks. This is hard and important work, and you can take the time it deserves.

It's also important to keep in mind that a great deal of our knowing comes from looking at, exploring, and working with our feelings.

Here is one way of viewing what happens when we work our Fourth and Fifth Steps. We move from grief to learnings, unworthiness to worthiness, shame to affirmation, disgrace to discretion, self-sabotage to health, paralysis to respect, misuse to empowerment, and avoidance to responsibility. We do this one day at a time by consulting and working with our emotions.

# The Fourth and Fifth Steps

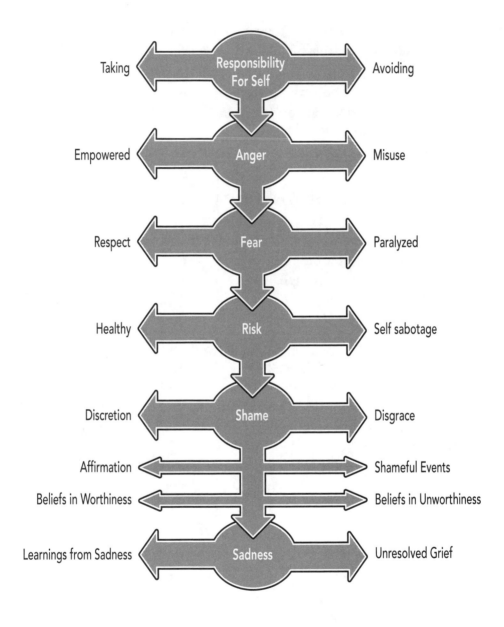

Now, proceed to your first Fourth Step inventory.

# Fourth Step Inventories

## Fourth Step Inventory: Avoiding Personal Responsibility

When taking Step Four, often the first feeling you get in touch with is discomfort. When people get uncomfortable about their behavior—especially where the potential for feeling real pain exists—they look for ways to protect themselves from the consequences of that behavior. Some of these ways are dysfunctional and self-destructive. These defensive manipulations lead us to avoid responsibility. Examples include blaming others, denial, dishonesty, intimidation, and rationalization. Sometimes you may even go to great lengths to make people in your life feel crazy. You may make up stories or act in other ways to distract or divert attention from your behavior. How have you avoided taking responsibility for your behavior? Give specific examples.

*Example:* I pretended Bill never told me about our appointment at school when the truth is, I forgot.

1. _____

   _____

   _____

2. _____

   _____

   _____

3. _____

   _____

   _____

4. _____

_____

_____

5. _____

_____

_____

6. _____

_____

_____

7. _____

_____

_____

8. _____

_____

_____

9. _____

_____

_____

10. _____

_____

_____

11. _____

_____

_____

12. _____

_____

_____

13. _____

_____

_____

14. _____

_____

_____

15. _____

_____

_____

16. _____

_____

_____

17. _____

_____

_____

18. _____

_____

_____

19. _____

_____

_____

20. _____

_____

_____

## Fourth Step Inventory: Taking Personal Responsibility

Sometimes you take responsibility for your discomfort. You can, for example, set boundaries about what you wish to talk about. Or you can express your discomfort and take responsibility for your behavior. In what ways have you clearly owned your behavior? Give specific examples.

*Example:* I admitted to Susan that I forgot our anniversary.

1. _____

_____

_____

2. _____

_____

_____

3. _____

_____

_____

4. _____

_____

_____

5. _____

_____

_____

6. _____

_____

_____

7. _____

_____

_____

8. _____

_____

_____

9. _____

_____

_____

10. _____
    _____
    _____

11. _____
    _____
    _____

12. _____
    _____
    _____

13. _____
    _____
    _____

14. _____
    _____
    _____

15. _____
    _____
    _____

16. _____
    _____
    _____

17. _____

_____

_____

18. _____

_____

_____

19. _____

_____

_____

20. _____

_____

_____

## Fourth Step Inventory: Misuse of Anger

Behind your defensive behavior there is a layer of anger. Perhaps you are angry because you got caught. Perhaps you are angry because you think people will leave you because of your behavior. You nurse grudges and resentments because you do not want to admit the damage you have done. At times you may hold on to anger so that you can stay connected to others you don't want to lose emotionally. Sometimes you might use anger to justify your addiction. In what ways have you misused your anger? Give specific examples.

*Example:* I used resentment toward my spouse to justify an affair.

1. _____

   _____

   _____

2. _____

   _____

   _____

3. _____

   _____

   _____

4. _____

   _____

   _____

5. _____

   _____

   _____

6. _____

   _____

   _____

7. _____

   _____

   _____

8. _____

   _____

   _____

9. _____

   _____

   _____

10. _____

    _____

    _____

11. _____

    _____

    _____

12. _____

    _____

    _____

13. _____

    _____

    _____

14. _____

    _____

    _____

15. _____

_____

_____

16. _____

_____

_____

17. _____

_____

_____

18. _____

_____

_____

19. _____

_____

_____

20. _____

_____

_____

**Fourth Step Inventory: Positive Expression of Anger**

Anger empowers people to resist manipulation and exploitation. Anger can give respect and dignity in abusive situations. Within an intimate relationship, anger is inevitable. Expressing anger becomes an act of trust that the other person is important and capable of handling the anger. No relationship can survive without appropriate anger. In what ways have you been respectful and assertive with your anger? Give specific examples.

*Example:* I got angry with my alcoholic father when he started being cruel to my children.

1. _____

   _____

   _____

2. _____

   _____

   _____

3. _____

   _____

   _____

4. _____

   _____

   _____

5. _____

   _____

   _____

6. _____

_____

_____

7. _____

_____

_____

8. _____

_____

_____

9. _____

_____

_____

10. _____

_____

_____

11. _____

_____

_____

12. _____

_____

_____

13. _____

_____

_____

14. _____

_____

_____

15. _____

_____

_____

16. _____

_____

_____

17. _____

_____

_____

18. _____

_____

_____

19. _____

_____

_____

20. _____

_____

_____

## Fourth Step Inventory: Paralyzed by Fear

Fear is the next layer of feelings. Fear can be immobilizing. When did you need to take action but did not? Make yourself vulnerable but did not? Take a risk but did not? Have you put off important tasks and discussions? In what ways have you compromised yourself by being stuck in your fear? Give specific examples.

*Example:* I was afraid to admit how frightened I was to leave my job—so no one understood.

1. _____

_____

_____

2. _____

_____

_____

3. _____

_____

_____

4. _____

_____

5. _____

_____

_____

6. _____

_____

_____

7. _____

_____

_____

8. _____

_____

_____

9. _____

_____

_____

10. _____

_____

_____

11. _____

_____

_____

12. _____

_____

_____

13. _____

_____

_____

14. _____

_____

_____

15. _____

_____

_____

16. _____

_____

_____

17. _____

_____

_____

18. _____

_____

_____

19. _____

_____

_____

20. _____

_____

_____

## Fourth Step Inventory: Respect for Fear

Fear serves as an important guide for your safety. Sometimes it helps you to avoid disasters and take care of yourself. When have you listened to your fear appropriately? Give specific examples.

*Example:* I knew it was not a good idea to date the guy I met at the airport this early in my recovery.

1. _____

_____

_____

2. _____

_____

_____

3. _____

_____

_____

4. _____

_____

_____

5. _____

_____

_____

6. _____

_____

_____

7. _____

_____

_____

8. _____

_____

_____

9. _____

_____

_____

10. _____

_____

_____

11. _____

_____

_____

12. _____

_____

_____

13. _____

_____

_____

14. _____

_____

_____

15. _____

_____

_____

16. _____

_____

_____

17. _____

_____

_____

18. _____

_____

_____

19. _____

_____

_____

20. _____

_____

_____

## Fourth Step Inventory: Falling into Self-sabotage

When we're stressed, challenged, or frightened, we may do things that get in our own way—or that outright sabotage us. The less attentive we are to our emotions, and the fewer efforts we make to learn what they are about, the most likely we are to create these problems.

Make a list of specific things you did that slowed you down, held you back, or scuttled opportunities for success. These can be things you did deliberately out of fear, or things you did without realizing it, out of inattention.

*Example:* I interviewed for a more interesting job with a much higher salary, but that would give me much more responsibility. The first interview went very well, but on the morning of the second interview I didn't pay attention to the time and arrived ten minutes late. The interviewers commented on my lateness, and I did not get the job.

1. _____

   _____

   _____

2. _____

   _____

   _____

3. _____

   _____

   _____

4. _____

   _____

   _____

5. _____

   _____

   _____

6. _____

   _____

   _____

7. _____

   _____

   _____

8. _____

_____

_____

9. _____

_____

_____

10. _____

_____

_____

11. _____

_____

_____

12. _____

_____

_____

13. _____

_____

_____

14. _____

_____

_____

15. _____

_____

_____

16. _____

_____

_____

17. _____

_____

_____

18. _____

_____

_____

19. _____

_____

_____

20. _____

_____

_____

**Fourth Step Inventory: Taking Healthy Risks**

Moments occur in which you have to set your fears aside and take significant risks. What risks have you taken for your own growth? Give specific examples.

*Example:* I had an idea about a new business and took the risk to try it.

1. _____

   _____

   _____

2. _____

   _____

   _____

3. _____

   _____

   _____

4. _____

   _____

   _____

5. _____

   _____

   _____

6. _____

_____

_____

7. _____

_____

_____

8. _____

_____

_____

9. _____

_____

_____

10. _____

_____

_____

11. _____

_____

_____

12. _____

_____

_____

13. _____

_____

_____

14. _____

_____

_____

15. _____

_____

_____

16. _____

_____

_____

17. _____

_____

_____

18. _____

_____

_____

19. _____

_____

_____

20. _____

_____

_____

## Fourth Step Inventory: Shameful Events

At an even deeper layer, addicts feel shame. You need to know when you have not lived up to your values or when you have failed to practice what you preach. Since you tell yourself that other people do not do what you did, you believe that if they found out, you would be rejected. You feel fundamentally embarrassed about yourself and unlovable. And the more shameful you feel, the more secretive you are.

A more realistic—and gentler—way of looking at your failures is to see that you are a limited human being who makes mistakes, who is lovable and forgivable. You must also remember the powerlessness and unmanageability of your illness. With these things in mind, in what ways have you not lived up to your own values? (Suggestion: A good guideline is to start with a list of the things you have kept secret—these are at the core of shame.) Remember, be specific.

*Example:* A major secret I have is . . . or, I feel really bad about . . .

1. _____

_____

_____

2. _____

_____

_____

3. _____

_____

_____

4. _____

_____

_____

5. _____

_____

_____

6. _____

_____

_____

7. _____

_____

_____

8. _____

_____

_____

9. _____

_____

_____

10. _____

_____

_____

11. _____

_____

_____

12. _____

_____

_____

13. _____

_____

_____

14. _____

_____

_____

15. _____

_____

_____

16. _____

_____

_____

17. _____

_____

_____

18. _____

_____

_____

19. _____

_____

_____

20. _____

_____

_____

**Fourth Step Inventory: Pride in Your Achievements**

As a balance, you need to account for your achievements. Think of those moments when you lived up to your values or followed through on what you said you would do. Don't forget those times when you were courageous or generous and exceeded your expectations. List those times when you were intimate, vulnerable, and caring. Don't forget to include your entry into your recovery program and getting this far in the workbook! In what do you take pride? Give specific examples.

*Example:* I feel good about how I supported my son when he was hurt last fall.

1. _____

_____

_____

2. _____

_____

_____

3. _____

_____

_____

4. _____

_____

_____

5. _____

_____

_____

6. _____

_____

_____

7. _____

_____

_____

8. _____

_____

_____

9. _____

_____

_____

10. _____

_____

_____

11. _____

_____

_____

12. _____

_____

_____

13. _____

_____

_____

14. _____

_____

_____

15. _____

_____

_____

16. _____

_____

_____

17. _____

_____

_____

18. _____

_____

_____

19. _____

_____

_____

20. _____

_____

_____

**Fourth Step Inventory: Losses and Painful Events**

Beneath shame, there is often a feeling of sadness. Many variations of sadness exist for anyone who has lived with addictive extremes. First, you grieve for all the losses: time, people, opportunities, and dreams. Second, your sorrow for those you have harmed may be quite overwhelming. Finally, there is your pain about how deeply you have been hurt by this illness. In what ways are you sad? What losses do you feel? Give specific examples in each category.

*Example:* I am sorry about all the times I missed being with my children.

1. _____

_____

_____

2. _____

_____

_____

3. _____

_____

_____

4. _____

_____

_____

5. _____

_____

_____

6. _____

_____

_____

7. _____

_____

_____

8. _____

_____

_____

9. _____

_____

_____

10. _____

_____

_____

I have pain about these events.

*Example:* I hurt because of my teacher's abuse of me.

1. _____

_____

_____

2. _____

_____

_____

3. _____

_____

_____

4. _____

_____

_____

5. _____

_____

_____

6. _____

_____

_____

7. _____

_____

_____

8. _____

_____

_____

9. _____

_____

_____

10. _____

_____

_____

## Fourth Step Inventory: Learning from Sadness

An old Buddhist saying suggests that suffering is "clinging to that which changes." Grief, sorrow, and pain simply are part of life—especially given your powerlessness over your illness and commitment to recovery. When you work through the feelings, they remain with you and add depth to who you are. You integrate new learnings. Despite the losses, your life is better than before. What gains have you made through your sadness? Give specific examples.

*Example:* I have learned I can live independently since my divorce.

1. _____

_____

_____

2. _____

_____

_____

3. _____

_____

_____

4. _____

_____

_____

5. _____

_____

_____

6. _____

_____

_____

7. _____

_____

_____

8. _____

_____

_____

9. _____

_____

_____

10. _____

_____

_____

11. _____

_____

_____

12. _____

_____

_____

13. _____

_____

_____

14. _____

_____

_____

15. _____

_____

_____

16. _____

_____

_____

17. _____

_____

_____

18. _____

_____

_____

19. _____

_____

_____

20. _____

_____

_____

### Fourth Step Inventory:
### Beliefs about Your Unworthiness

The final feeling you will reach through your Fourth Step is that of loneliness. Loneliness is created by feelings of unworthiness that separate us from others. Addicts and coaddicts have lost the most important relationship of all—the relationship with themselves. How you treat yourself becomes the lens through which you view others. Fidelity to oneself results in faithfulness to others. Integrity with oneself generates trust of others. At our core, we are alone. So we each need to learn to enjoy, love, trust, and care for our self.

A word of caution: This final layer may be the most difficult to be honest about. You might find all kinds of ways to resist doing this last part thoroughly. Since your relationship with yourself is the foundation of your recovery, take time to face this part of the inventory squarely.

You need to list beliefs you have about your own unworthiness— that is, about being a bad person. Seeing oneself as a flawed human being is core to the belief system of all addicts and coaddicts. Some of these faulty beliefs are easily identified as not true. Others are more difficult to determine. List all you can think of.

*Example:* I am a deceptive person.

1. _____

_____

_____

2. _____

_____

_____

3. _____

_____

_____

4. _____

_____

_____

5. _____

_____

_____

6. _____

_____

_____

7. _____

_____

_____

8. _____

_____

_____

9. _____

_____

_____

10. _____

_____

_____

11. _____

_____

_____

12. _____

_____

_____

13. _____

_____

_____

14. _____

_____

_____

15. _____

_____

_____

16. _____

_____

_____

17. _____

_____

_____

18. _____

_____

_____

19. _____

_____

_____

20. _____

_____

_____

## Fourth Step Inventory: Self-hatred

After listing the beliefs you hold about your unworthiness, you need to be as explicit as possible about how deep the roots of your self-hatred go. As an addict, you have become an expert at beating yourself up. What things are you hardest on yourself about? Make a list of examples of self-hatred, including ways you have punished yourself, hurt yourself, put yourself down, or sold yourself out. Do not forget to include fantasies of terrible things happening to you because you somehow deserve them.

*Example:* I take projects almost to the end and don't finish them.

1. _____

   _____

   _____

2. _____

   _____

   _____

3. _____

   _____

   _____

4. _____

   _____

   _____

5. _____

   _____

   _____

6. _____

_____

_____

7. _____

_____

_____

8. _____

_____

_____

9. _____

_____

_____

10. _____

_____

_____

11. _____

_____

_____

12. _____

_____

_____

13. _____

_____

_____

14. _____

_____

_____

15. _____

_____

_____

16. _____

_____

_____

17. _____

_____

_____

18. _____

_____

_____

19. _____

_____

_____

20. _____

_____

_____

## Fourth Step Inventory: Self-affirmations

An affirmation is a statement about some goodness in you. Spend some time thinking about the many positive qualities you possess. How are you enjoyable, loving, caring, and trustworthy? This may also be a difficult task. Sometimes, early in recovery, good things are more evident to others than they are to you. Ask for help. When you have completed your list, you might want to make a voice recording of yourself reading it. You will then have a ready-made series of affirmations when you need them.

*Example:* I am a person of great courage.

1. I am _____

2. I am _____

3. I am _____

4. I am _____

5. I am _____

6. I am _____

7. I am _____

8. I am _____

9. I am _____

10. I am _____

11. I am _____

12. I am _____

13. I am _____

14. I am _____

15. I am _____

16. I am _____

17. I am _____

18. I am _____

19. I am _____

20. I am _____

21. I am _____

22. I am _____

23. I am _____

24. I am _____

25. I am _____

26. I am _____

27. I am _____

28. I am _____

29. I am _____

30. I am _____

## Reflections on the Fourth Step

The difficult road is the road of conversion, the conversion from loneliness into solitude. Instead of running away from our loneliness and trying to forget or deny it, we have to protect it and turn it into a fruitful solitude. To live a spiritual life, we must first find the courage to enter into the desert of our loneliness and to change it by gentle and persistent efforts into a garden of solitude. This requires not only courage, but also a strong faith. As difficult as it is to believe that the dry, desolate desert can yield endless varieties of flowers, it is equally difficult to imagine that our loneliness is hiding unknown beauty. The movement from loneliness to solitude, however, is the beginning of any spiritual life because it is the movement from the restless senses to the restful spirit, from the outward-reaching cravings to the inward-reaching search, from the fearful clinging to the fearless play.

— Henri Nouwen
*Reaching Out*

Read the words of Henri Nouwen above and reflect on the process of going through the layers of your Fourth Step.

Record your reactions to facing your own loneliness.

_____

_____

_____

_____

_____

_____

# Sharing Step Five

## Suggestions for the Turning Point

Successful Fifth Steps come from sharing your written inventory with another person who will recognize and note the sources of greatest feeling or the places where you were stuck. As consultant as well as witness, the person who hears your Fifth Step will help you over the difficult parts of your story.

Remember also that the whole Fifth Step does not have to be done in one session. Some people who listen to Fifth Steps regularly recommend two to three sessions as opposed to a marathon event in which you share all your work at one time. Don't forget the gentleness of the path you are on.

Addicts and coaddicts often say that completing the Fifth Step was a real turning point in their recovery, that the first three Steps took on new meaning, and that they felt anchored in the program. The Fifth Step does provide special support in the person who hears your story at perhaps the most difficult point in the program. The loneliness of the Fourth Step becomes an opportunity for reaching out. A special intimacy occurs when someone accepts you even though he or she knows the very worst things about you. That experience of closeness can be duplicated as you deepen bonds with others in your life.

Spaces are provided on the following pages for you and the person with whom you have shared your Fifth Step to record your reactions, your feelings, and the progress you have made. Have fun with it together.

My feelings in sharing my Fifth Step:

_____

_____

_____

_____

_____

_____

_____

_____

_____

_____

_____

_____

_____

_____

_____

_____

_____

Your name: _____

Date: _____

My feelings in hearing your Fifth Step:

_____

_____

_____

_____

_____

_____

_____

_____

_____

_____

_____

_____

_____

_____

_____

_____

_____

Your name: _____

Date: _____

## Fifth Step Reconciliation Rite

A reader from California said he thought something was missing from the Fourth and Fifth Step exercise, but he didn't know what. When we received this gift of a reconciliation rite from an Episcopal priest, it seemed to provide the missing piece. In the priest's letter, she told us she uses it in all of the Fifth Step work that she does.

A Fifth Step is done to reestablish friendship and harmony with oneself and one's Higher Power.

- Think of one word to symbolize all you have disclosed.

- Hold out your hands to form a cup, as if someone were going to pour water into your hands.

- Say the word that represents your Fifth Step. Imagine the word resting in your hands.

- Slowly pour your Fifth Step from your hands onto the ground, as if you are letting water pour from your hands. Brush your hands as you would to brush off sand.

- If you are doing this in the presence of your guide or your group, have them say to you, while they place a hand on you, "That which has kept you divided within yourself is gone. You are whole."

- Repeat the phrase for yourself, "That which has kept me divided within myself is gone. I am whole."

- Allow yourself to feel your feelings and meditate a few moments longer.

The feeling of being forgiven by a Higher Power can lead to self-forgiveness. Forgiving oneself begins the process of healing our brokenness.

Record your thoughts and feelings:

_____

_____

_____

_____

_____

_____

_____

_____

_____

_____

_____

_____

_____

_____

_____

_____

_____

_____

_____

_____

## Reflections on the Fifth Step

It strikes us when, year after year, the longed-for perfection of life does not appear, when the old compulsions reign within us as they have for decades, when despair destroys all joy and courage. Sometimes at that moment a wave of light breaks through our darkness, and it is as though a voice is saying, "You are accepted." YOU ARE ACCEPTED, accepted by that which is greater than you and the name of which you do not know. Do not ask for the name now, perhaps you will know it later. Do not try to do anything, perhaps later you will do much. Do not seek for anything, do not perform anything, do not intend anything, SIMPLY ACCEPT THE FACT THAT YOU ARE ACCEPTED.

— Paul Tillich, *The Courage to Be*

Read the Paul Tillich quote above and reflect on the acceptance you experienced from doing your Fifth Step.

Record your thoughts and feelings here:

_____

_____

_____

_____

_____

_____

_____

_____

_____

_____

_____

_____

_____

_____

_____

_____

_____

The Fourth and Fifth Steps teach us about the importance of engaging our feelings. Unexamined feelings feed our addictions; honestly examining our feelings helps us heal from addiction.

As we work the Twelve Steps and explore our feelings, we get better at determining when they can help us and when they can't. Our discernment improves, and so does our decision making.

At the beginning of this book we noted the importance of an inner observer who monitors and recognizes what's going on in our brain. Neuroscientists and therapists agree that a healthy inner observer can help us to maintain our emotional balance, build empathy, and generally stay sane. However, although our brain is wired to create and house an inner observer, it doesn't just appear on its own; we have to develop it through effort and attention. Over time, working the Twelve Steps naturally creates an inner observer who is discerning, honest, and wise.

# Step Six

*Were entirely ready to have God remove
all these defects of character.*

# Step Seven

*Humbly asked Him to remove our shortcomings.*

THE FOURTH AND FIFTH Steps revealed two types of short-comings. The first are defects that you originally learned as survival tools. You developed many of your defenses as a way to cope with growing up. For example, isolation may have been the only way to cope with abuse in your family. Now that you are in recovery, you can discard dysfunctional ways of taking care of yourself. You can embrace new, healthy ways. In that sense, this stage of recovery parallels giving birth—a wondrous, painful, and, at times ugly, process. The exercises in this chapter are designed to help you remove your shortcomings, use a lifestyle inventory to bring your life into manageability, and develop relapse prevention tools to help you stay on the gentle path of recovery.

One thing that can stop this process is relapse—which brings us to the other types of shortcomings, the quirks of the addict within. These quirks are grandiosity, pride, willfulness, jealousy, depression, suicidal preoccupation—those aspects of yourself that combine to make you vulnerable to your addiction and coaddiction. These are the shortcomings that can return you to the compulsive spirals you were in before you entered the program. Some of these shortcomings may have helped you survive in the past, but now they are a gateway to disaster.

Several tasks can help you with the Sixth and Seventh Steps:

**Affirmations**—Steps Six and Seven ask us to be willing to remove our defects. These affirmations are written to help you let go of old, familiar habits and attitudes and develop new and positive character strengths.

**Step Six: Removing Character Defects**—Part of our work on Steps Six and Seven helps to identify character defects. In this task, you make a list of those shortcomings you are willing to turn over to your Higher Power and the positive qualities to replace them with. For example, if dishonesty is your shortcoming, honesty is what you are working toward. Transforming weaknesses into strengths is what recovery is all about.

**Seventh Step Meditation**—This exercise helps you visualize your life without defects and shortcomings. It helps you develop a positive vision of the person you are becoming in recovery. You compose a meditation or prayer to help you remember that your Higher Power can help in this process.

**Personal Craziness Index**—Another task in working these two Steps is to fill out a Personal Craziness Index (PCI, pronounced "picky"), a playful tool with a serious intent—to prevent relapse. The leading cause of relapse is lifestyle imbalance—being overstretched or overextended. At these times the quirks of the addict within are immediately available.

**When Crises Occur**—Under stress it is easy to forget our new recovery behavior tools. That is why it is so important to recognize a crisis when it happens and respond with the new behaviors and inner resources you are learning about.

## Affirmations

Affirmations can help us change our behavior. We can replace unhealthy messages with messages we select. Each affirmation is written in the present—as if you are already accomplishing it. Even though it may not be a reality for you today, you need to "act as if." In time, telling yourself positive messages will become a familiar habit. Recovery is really a retraining program. It's about learning new ways to relate to ourselves and others. As our attitudes improve, so do our lives.

Read these affirmations to yourself or make a voice recording and play it back. Pause a few seconds after each. Let the words sink deep into your consciousness. For greatest effect, repeat the exercise often.

- *I enjoy taking responsibility for those things that order my life and make my life free of hassle.*

- *I allow others to take responsibility for their lives.*

- *I enjoy taking care of my body.*

- *Exercise makes me feel healthy, strong, and happy.*

- *Good nutrition allows my body to maximize its potential.*

- *I do everything I need to keep myself healthy, fit, and feeling good.*

- *I get the rest and relaxation I need.*

- *I am financially responsible. I earn more than I spend.*

- *Each day I become more organized in all areas of my life.*

- *I accept that I can make mistakes and still keep trying.*

- *I am grateful for a sense of humor that helps me know that I am human.*

- *I meet all of my obligations. I accept only those obligations I can meet.*

- *Being on time is easy for me. I am always on time. I have the courage to change.*

- *I take risks that will help me grow in positive, healthy ways.*

- *I value my emotions as a cherished part of me, a part to get to know, understand, and love more each day.*

- *My interpersonal relationships are healthy, open, and honest.*

- *I maintain the rituals of my spirituality.*

- *I always allow enough time to get where I am going. I am responsible, relaxed, and organized in getting to and from my destinations.*

- *I use my time, my money, my energy, and all of my resources responsibly.*

Create additional affirmations that are meaningful to you:

_____

_____

_____

_____

_____

_____

_____

_____

_____

_____

_____

_____

Throughout this book you have been reading, repeating, and creating your own affirmations. Now you can begin making them a regular part of your recovery and your life.

Look back at all the affirmations you've worked with so far: "Affirmations" in Step One; "Spirituality Affirmations" in Steps Two and Three; and "Self-affirmations" in Steps Four and Five. As you read through them, pick out four to ten that you find especially helpful or meaningful, and write them down on a piece of paper. Then do one or more of the following things with that piece of paper:

- Post it somewhere prominent in your home—on a mirror, your fridge, or a bulletin board. If you like, repeat the affirmations aloud as you cook or dress or put on makeup.

- Carry it in your wallet or purse.

- Tape it to the dashboard of your car.

- Post it in a visible spot in your workplace.

- Create your own personal "God box": a container filled with inspiring, hopeful writings and objects. Put the list of affirmations in this box. Open the God box in times of despair to remind you that all the hard work you've done in recovery has not been wasted.

You can also make a recording of yourself reading these affirmations aloud. Play this recording just before you fall asleep—or whenever you want to encourage yourself to do and be your best.

The point is to take these affirmations out into your life, so that they serve as regular reminders of your commitment to recovery—and so you can easily access them at critical moments.

## Step Six: Removing Character Defects

Bryan, from Texas, uses *A Gentle Path through the Twelve Steps* with the people he sponsors. He recognizes that addicts and coaddicts tend to feel deprived when they think of giving up something or having it removed. It is important to remember that sobriety is not about depriving oneself, but about learning how to do things differently. This exercise is designed to help you replace unhealthy defects and shortcomings with healthy behaviors.

List below your character defects or shortcomings as you see them. As you list each one, focus on the positive it can become, and list that positive quality in the parallel column.

| Defects and shortcomings I am willing to turn over | Qualities I wish to work toward |
|---|---|
| *Example:* Dishonesty | *Example:* Honesty |
| 1. | 1. |
| 2. | 2. |
| 3. | 3. |
| 4. | 4. |
| 5. | 5. |

6.                                6.

7.                                7.

8.                                8.

9.                                9.

10.                              10.

11.                              11.

12.                              12.

13.                              13.

14.                              14.

15.                              15.

## Seventh Step Meditation

Reflecting on your shortcomings, compose a prayer or meditation that you can use in times of stress to ask for help with your short comings. Suggestion: Include reminders of how desperate you were in your addiction, of your commitment to recovery, and of your powerlessness.

_____

_____

_____

_____

_____

_____

_____

_____

_____

_____

_____

_____

_____

_____

_____

_____

_____

_____

Lifestyle imbalance makes the addict vulnerable to relapse in the following ways.

**Feelings of entitlement.** When overextended, addicts and co-addicts seek addictive nurturing because they are so depleted. They tell themselves they are entitled and deserve it, rationalizing the return to self-destructive patterns.

**Increase of cravings.** When there is not enough time to take care of oneself, urges to repeat the old cycle multiply. Obsessional thinking is a relief to current stress.

**Return of denial.** In periods of imbalance, euphoric recall makes old cycles seem attractive again. Deluded thinking avoids the probable consequences of a return to previous behavior.

**Reduction of coping ability.** When overextended, your ability to cope with problems is diminished. Bad decisions and poor problem solving further compound the crises in an unmanageable life.

**Participation in high-risk behaviors.** During times of stress, destructive situations, persons, and events that are normally avoided become attractive. The reality of unsafe behavior becomes distorted by overextension.

When you were in high school or college, you may have participated in an athletic program. Preparing for the stress of competition is called training. An athlete prepares for a stressful event (a match, game, or tournament) by observing a training program that creates extra margins of endurance and strength and that develops skills for the event. Similarly, addicts and coaddicts in a recovery program are training to participate in life. You know that you are going to experience stress, and you must prepare for that. The Twelve Steps will help you learn the necessary skills, but you also need to develop a lifestyle that builds up reserves of strength and endurance.

Think of your life as having an addiction set point—the point at which the imbalance leaves you vulnerable to addiction, when you are too stressed or overextended to maintain your recovery.

**Lifestyle Balance**        **Lifestyle Imbalance**

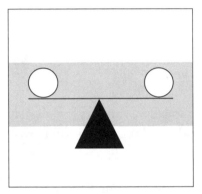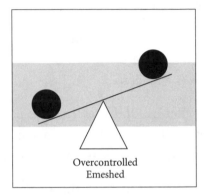

Overcontrolled
Emeshed

Well prepared to handle       Vulnerable to Addiction
life's problems and
maintain recovery

By developing a sense of what your own personal set point is, you can be alert to maintaining the balance that makes you less vulnerable to the quirks of your addict. The PCI described below will help you develop some criteria for recognizing when you have passed that point of sanity and are at risk. The PCI thus can become a set of training guidelines under which you train for anticipated stress. In addition, by keeping track of your own PCI for a period of time, you will get better and better at maintaining lifestyle balance and having some fun.

# Personal Craziness Index

### Part One—Preparation

The Personal Craziness Index (PCI) is based on two assumptions:

1. **Craziness first appears in routine, simple behaviors that support lifestyle balance.**

2. **Behavioral signs will occur in patterns involving different parts of our lives.**

Thus, we can be caught up in issues of cosmic importance and not notice that our checking account is overdrawn. If our checking account is overdrawn, we are probably out of socks as well, because we have not done our laundry. If this pattern is pervasive, there is a risk that our lives will become emotionally bankrupt as well—cosmic issues notwithstanding.

Addicts and coaddicts are particularly vulnerable to the insanity of loss of reality from having neglected the basics. "Keep it simple" and "One day at a time" are not shopworn clichés, but guidelines borne out by the experience of many recovering people. The PCI helps you to remember what you need to do each day. It helps you establish good recovery habits. Without a structured process to keep you on track, cunning and baffling self-destructive behavior patterns will return. You'll also find the PCI helpful during periods of stress and vulnerability.

The process of creating your own PCI is designed to be as value-free as possible. Each person uses his or her own criteria to develop the index. In other words, you are asked to generate behavioral signs (or critical incidents) which, through your own experience, you have learned to identify as danger signs or warnings that you are losing it, getting out of hand, or burning out. Thus, you will judge yourself by your own standards.

You may change the items in the index as you progress in your recovery. The following are ten areas of personal behavior suggested as sources of danger signs. Please add some of your own, if you wish.

**1. Physical Health.** The ultimate insanity is to not take care of our bodies. Without our bodies, we have nothing, yet we seem to have little time for physical conditioning. Examples are being overweight, abusing cigarettes or caffeine, not getting regular exercise, eating junk food, getting insufficient sleep, and having a lingering sickness. When do you know that you are not taking care of your body? Give at least three examples.

_____

_____

_____

_____

_____

**2. Transportation.** How people get from place to place is often a statement about their lifestyles. Take, for example, a car owner who seldom comes to a full stop, routinely exceeds the speed limit, runs out of gas, does not check the oil, puts off needed repairs, has not cleaned out the back seat in three months, and averages three speeding tickets and ten parking tickets a year. Or the bus rider who always misses the bus, never has change, forgets his or her briefcase on the bus, and so forth. What transportation behaviors indicate that your life is getting out of control? Give at least three examples.

_____

_____

_____

_____

**3. Environment.** To not have time to do your personal chores is a comment on the order of your life. Consider the home in which plants go unwatered, fish unfed, grocery supplies depleted, laundry not done or put away, cleaning neglected, dishes unwashed. What are ways in which you neglect your home? Give at least three examples.

_____

_____

_____

_____

_____

_____

**4. Work.** Chaos at work is risky for recovery. Signs of chaotic behavior are phone calls not returned within twenty-four hours, chronic lateness for appointments, being behind in promised work, an unmanageable in-basket, and too many irons in the fire. When your life is unmanageable at work, what are your behaviors? Give at least three examples.

_____

_____

_____

_____

_____

_____

**5. Interests.** What are some positive interests besides work that give you perspective on the world? Music, reading, photography, fishing, and gardening are examples. What are you neglecting to do when you are overextended? Give at least three examples.

_____

_____

_____

_____

_____

**6. Social Life.** Think of friends in your social network who provide you with significant support. (These should be friends, not your partner or family members.) When you become isolated, alienated, or disconnected from them, what do you typically do? Give at least three examples.

_____

_____

_____

_____

_____

**7. Family/Significant Others.** When you are disconnected from those closest to you, what is your typical reaction? For example, are you silent, overtly hostile, or passive-aggressive? Give at least three examples.

_____

_____

_____

_____

_____

_____

**8. Finances.** We handle our financial resources much as we do our emotional ones. Thus, when your checking account is unbalanced, or worse, overdrawn, or bills are overdue, or there is no cash in your pocket, or you are spending more than you earn, your financial overextension may parallel your emotional bankruptcy. What are the indications when you are financially overextended? Give at least three examples.

_____

_____

_____

_____

_____

_____

**9. Spiritual Life and Personal Reflection.** Spirituality can be diverse and can include such practices as meditation, yoga, and prayer. Personal reflection includes keeping a personal journal, working the Twelve Step program with daily readings, and getting therapy. What sources of routine personal reflection do you neglect when you are overextended? Give at least three examples.

_____

_____

_____

_____

_____

**10. Other Addictions or Symptom Behaviors.** Compulsive behaviors that have negative consequences are symptomatic of your general well-being or the state of your overall recovery. When you watch inordinate amounts of TV, overeat, bite your nails—any habit you feel bad about afterward—these can be signs of burnout or possible relapse. Symptom behaviors are evidence of overextension, such as forgetfulness, slips of the tongue, and jealousy. What negative addiction or symptom behaviors are present when you are on the edge? Give at least three examples.

_____

_____

_____

_____

_____

_____

## Part Two—Recording Your PCI

The PCI is effective only when a careful record is maintained. Recording your daily progress in conjunction with regular journal keeping will help you to keep focused on priorities that keep life manageable, work on program efforts a day at a time, expand your knowledge of personal patterns, and provide a warning in periods of vulnerability to self-destructive cycles or addictive relapse.

From the thirty or more signs of personal craziness you recorded, choose the seven that are most critical for you. At the end of each day, review the list of seven key signs and count the ones you did that day, giving each behavior one point. Record your total for that day in the space provided on the chart. If you fail to record the number of points for each day, that day receives an automatic score of 7. (If you cannot even do your score, you are obviously out of balance.) At the end of the week, total your seven daily scores and make an X on the graph. Pause and reflect on where you are in your recovery. Chart your progress over a twelve-week period.

My seven key signs of personal craziness:

1. _____

2. _____

3. _____

4. _____

5. _____

6. _____

7. _____

## PCI Chart

| Day | Week | 1 | 2 | 3 | 4 | 5 | 6 | 7 | 8 | 9 | 10 | 11 | 12 |
|---|---|---|---|---|---|---|---|---|---|---|---|---|---|
| Sunday | | | | | | | | | | | | | |
| Monday | | | | | | | | | | | | | |
| Tuesday | | | | | | | | | | | | | |
| Wednesday | | | | | | | | | | | | | |
| Thursday | | | | | | | | | | | | | |
| Friday | | | | | | | | | | | | | |
| Saturday | | | | | | | | | | | | | |
| **Weekly Total** | | | | | | | | | | | | | |

## PCI Graph

| | | 1 | 2 | 3 | 4 | 5 | 6 | 7 | 8 | 9 | 10 | 11 | 12 |
|---|---|---|---|---|---|---|---|---|---|---|---|---|---|
| 50 | | | | | | | | | | | | | |
| | Very High Risk | 48 | | | | | | | | | | | |
| | | 46 | | | | | | | | | | | |
| | | 44 | | | | | | | | | | | |
| | | 42 | | | | | | | | | | | |
| 40 | | | | | | | | | | | | | |
| | High Risk | 38 | | | | | | | | | | | |
| | | 36 | | | | | | | | | | | |
| | | 34 | | | | | | | | | | | |
| | | 32 | | | | | | | | | | | |
| 30 | | | | | | | | | | | | | |
| | Medium Risk | 28 | | | | | | | | | | | |
| | | 26 | | | | | | | | | | | |
| | | 24 | | | | | | | | | | | |
| | | 22 | | | | | | | | | | | |
| 20 | | | | | | | | | | | | | |
| | Stable Solidity | 18 | | | | | | | | | | | |
| | | 16 | | | | | | | | | | | |
| | | 14 | | | | | | | | | | | |
| | | 12 | | | | | | | | | | | |
| 10 | | | | | | | | | | | | | |
| | Optimum Health | 8 | | | | | | | | | | | |
| | | 6 | | | | | | | | | | | |
| | | 4 | | | | | | | | | | | |
| | | 2 | | | | | | | | | | | |
| 0 | | | | | | | | | | | | | |

# Part Three—Interpretation of the PCI

A guideline for understanding your score is suggested below.

**Optimum Health**
**0–9**

Knows limits; has clear priorities; behavior congruent with values; rooted in diversity; supportive; has established a personal system; balanced, orderly, resolves crises quickly; capacity to sustain spontaneity; shows creative discipline.

**Stable Solidity**
**10–19**

Recognizes human limits; does not pretend to be more than he or she is; maintains most boundaries; well ordered; typically feels competent; feels supported; able to weather crisis.

**Medium Risk**
**20–29**

Slipping; often rushed, can't get it all in; no emotional margin for crisis; vulnerable to slip into old patterns; typically lives as if has inordinate influence over others and/or feels inadequate.

**High Risk**
**30–39**

Living in extremes (overactive or inactive); relationships abbreviated; feels and is irresponsible; constantly has reasons for not following through; lives one way, talks another; works hard to catch up.

**Very High Risk**
**40–49**

Usually pursuing self-destructive behavior; often totally into mission, cause, or project; blames others for failures; seldom produces on time; controversial in community; success vs. achievement oriented.

## Part Four—PCI Meditation

Use the PCI as a gentle nudge to move you in the direction you want to go. As addicts and coaddicts we can get compulsive and obsessive about almost anything—self-improvement included. One coaddict who uses *A Gentle Path through the Twelve Steps* described her first attempt at using the PCI. She was determined to do it right and put her life in order—once and for all. Finances had always been her greatest area of shame, so she spent two days designing a complete budget. The computerized spreadsheet listed all her income and all the bills that would be paid on each payday for the next two years. This was a good attempt on her part to put her finances in order. Unfortunately, the two days she spent doing the budget were April 14 and 15. In spending all the time on her spreadsheets, she forgot to file her taxes. Following is some advice to stay on the gentle path and yet work toward your goals.

- **Choose to do the inventory for a specific amount of time,** such as twelve weeks, or any time period that has a specific beginning and ending. After that time, review the process and decide to extend the time or do spot-check inventories each month, each quarter, or around holidays or significant anniversary dates. The thing we know about the inventory is that it modifies behavior. If you are going to have to report on yourself every night, you will find yourself behaving in a manner that will make it comfortable for you to report on yourself.

- **Be patient with yourself.** To change after years of compulsive behavior is a large task. Allow yourself the luxury of making mistakes. Even taking small steps toward balance provides a sense of satisfaction.

- **Accept yourself.** Remember your sense of humor. Be able to laugh at some of the situations that you find yourself in, but then go on and do what you can. Accept the imperfect.

- **Accept that working on your boundaries is a process—not a destination.** Set those PCI parameters as boundaries of healthy behavior—a goal to work toward. Later, when those goals have been achieved, you will want to redo the PCI and set new parameters.

- **Talk to your recovering friends about your progress and your failures.** They will be your mirror to help you see when your compulsivity is getting out of control.

- **Understand that things will change.** There is as much challenge in trying to achieve balance as there was when we were constantly facing the chaos of living on the edge. The PCI is designed to give you a stable base so that when the unexpected comes up you won't be thrown off your balance.

## When Crises Occur—Acknowledge the Chaos

Crises occur for all of us. And they seem to happen all at once, no matter how much effort we have put in. One night, flying home after a business trip, I had several simultaneous crises happening. At 30,000 feet there was little I could do. So I started to write down things I have learned about facing the inevitable crises in my life. Writing on the back of a plane ticket, I came up with fifteen action steps and five rules to remember:

**Action Steps**

1. Be gentle. It's an act of trust.

2. Trust yourself. Intuition is your brain working behind your back.

3. Get help. Sometimes things are too much.

4. Create space for yourself—use environment, time, and boundaries.

5. Allow yourself to retreat or cocoon for a time. Use that solitude for transformation, not just survival.

6. Embrace your antagonists. Struggle, anger, and disagreements lead to renewal.

7. Admit mistakes, including the ones no one else would know.

8. Keep focused. Grandiosity works only for the messianic.

9. Stop doing things that don't work. Trying harder only creates shame.

10. Sustain your visions. You will become your images.

11. Avoid catastrophizing. A strong grip on reality helps you, as well as others.

12. Finish things now. Incomplete transactions make for obsession.

13. Care for your body. It is the primary spiritual act.

14. Act to contain disasters. If too late, watch.

15. Plan for surprises. Only victims are surprised.

**Rules to Remember**

1. Fairness is not an issue. Reality is.

2. Fights and problems that repeat mean trouble. The issue is probably not the issue.

3. Blaming others is self-indulgent. Integrity exists only in self-responsibility.

4. Competing passions maintain life balance. Have hobbies.

5. Crises are. That's all.

6. Focus and humility go together.

A few words on Rule 6: We are happiest when we use our abilities, are good at what we do, and achieve something meaningful. Each of these requires focus. When we pursue too many things, or try to do too much, or let ourselves be pulled in too many directions, we lose our focus. As a result, our energy scatters, we achieve less, we may perform less well, and our life gets out of balance.

# Reflections on the
# Sixth and Seventh Steps

Beyond a wholesome discipline,
  be gentle with yourself.

You are a child of the universe, no less than the trees
  and the stars; you have a right to be here.

And whether or not it is clear to you, no doubt the
  universe is unfolding as it should.

— Max Ehrmann
*Desiderata*

Reflect on the words above and think of what gentleness you need for yourself at this point. While you turn over your imperfections, it helps to remember your goodness and acknowledge the higher order.

Record your thoughts.

_____

_____

_____

_____

_____

_____

_____

The Sixth and Seventh Steps teach us that stopping our addictive behavior is the beginning of recovery, not the goal. We need to look at everything in our life that has supported the process of addiction, and we need to make changes that support our recovery. In short, we need to re-engineer our lives, not just cease one form of harmful behavior. The Twelve Steps provide a blueprint for this re-engineering.

Addiction is not our only problem, or even our central one. Over the years, deeper issues have supported and encouraged the addiction—yet the drama of addiction has obscured those issues. They are cracks in our soul that we need to heal.

These cracks aren't mere metaphor. As we've seen, addicts literally have holes in their brains—physical areas of impaired function—created over time by their addictions.

The brain is always trying to save us time and effort, so it streamlines things to keep us from having to think about them. For example, if you're driving on the freeway to a meeting and you come to the exit for your home, you may take that exit even though it's the wrong one, because your brain is cued to take it automatically. It's created a habitual mental shortcut for you.

Our brain is full of such shortcuts. Some of these are helpful, but the ones created around our addiction are not. They are the source of much of our stinking thinking.

In recovery, we re-examine how we've designed each of our mental shortcuts and how they unconsciously push us toward certain decisions and actions. Then, by being intentional and focused, we change those decisions and actions; we create new patterns of thinking and acting.

Intention and mindfulness are at the core of this process. When we focus on making specific changes, we create the deepest neural pathways that support our new ways of thinking and acting. This is why therapy works. In his book *Flow*, psychologist Mihaly Csikszentmihalyi explains that as we focus on core issues and work to continuously improve, our brain heals. It also finds this process rewarding—so we become happier.

This process never ends. There's never a time when there's nothing more to learn and no more brain rewiring to do. There are always things to work on, always ways to improve.

This process also creates a feedback loop. When we are mindful about our thoughts, we become more mindful about the actions that result from them. And when we are mindful about our actions, we also become more mindful about the thoughts that lead to them.

# Step Eight

*Made a list of all persons we had harmed,
and became willing to make amends to them all.*

# Step Nine

*Made direct amends to such people wherever possible,
except when to do so would injure them or others.*

DR. SEUSS EXPLAINS a Ninth Step in *Bartholomew and the Oobleck*.
That story is paraphrased here:

> They still talk about it in the kingdom of Didd as "The-Year-
> the-King-Got-Angry-with-the-Sky." You see, in the King's
> grandiosity, he had decided that he was tired of the same four
> things coming down from the sky: snow, fog, sunshine, and
> rain. He wanted something NEW to come down from the sky.
> And he had his way. He got what he wanted when he wanted it.
> He called his spooky magicians, and with magic words they
> made it happen. It rained oobleck! Green, gooey, molasses-like
> stuff that stuck to everyone and wouldn't let go. The entire
> kingdom was paralyzed. Birds stuck to their nests, the royal
> musicians stuck to their instruments, the bell to warn the citi-
> zens was silenced by the green, yucky stuff. And the king sat on
> his throne, his royal crown stuck to his royal head.
>
> Finally, Bartholomew Cubbins could hold his tongue no
> longer. "It's going to keep on falling," he shouted, "until your
> whole great marble palace tumbles down! So don't waste your

time saying foolish magic words. YOU ought to be saying some plain, simple words!"

"*Simple* words? What do you mean, boy?"

"I mean," said Bartholomew, "this is all your fault! Now, the least you can do is say the simple words, 'I'm sorry.'"

No one had ever talked to the king like this before.

"What!" he bellowed. "ME . . . ME say 'I'm sorry!' Kings never say 'I'm sorry!'"

"But you're sitting in oobleck up to your chin. And so is everyone else in your land. And if you won't even say you're sorry, you're no sort of king at all!"

But then Bartholomew heard a great, deep sob. The old King was crying! "You're right! It is all my fault! And I am sorry! I'm awfully, awfully sorry!"

And the moment the King spoke those words, something happened.

Maybe there was magic in those simple words "I'm sorry."

Maybe there was magic in those simple words "It's all my fault."

Maybe there was, and maybe there wasn't. But they say that as soon as the old King spoke them, the sun began to shine and all the oobleck that was stuck on all the people and on all the animals of the Kingdom of Didd just simply, quietly melted away.

Saying "I'm sorry" is difficult, so we have developed several tools to help you through your Eighth and Ninth Steps.

**Worksheet**—This exercise will help you identify those you have harmed and how they were harmed.

**Story exercise, "The Healer Within"**—This guided imagery is designed to help you tap your inner resources for the wisdom and strength to heal yourself.

**Affirmations**—Affirmations will gently remind you of your strength for your Eighth and Ninth Step journey.

**Meditation**—This meditation will help enhance your ability to choose a new future and give you the inner discernment you need to walk the gentle path of recovery.

Besides asking for help from your Higher Power for your shortcomings, you can act on your own to mend the harm you have caused as part of your illness. In Step Eight you identify people harmed, and in Step Nine you actually make the amends necessary. When finished with Step Nine, you will have done all you can and then you can turn over any remaining shame and guilt. The principles of forgiveness and restitution will become an ongoing part of living your life.

Reflecting on all levels of your awareness is very important to a thorough Eighth Step. When making your list of the persons you have harmed, consider the following:

**The name of the person who has been harmed.** Don't concentrate only on those people who are closest to you. Harm was done in casual relationships and acquaintanceships, as well.

**Memories of harm done.** Record the specifics that you remember about the harm, including your behavior and the other person's reactions. Include facial expressions, tones of voice, circumstances, or anything that will make clear what happened.

**Thoughts about the harm.** Ask yourself what you think about the situation now. Do you have reflections or interpretations about the harm?

**Feelings about the harm.** Acknowledge the pain, anger, shame, guilt, and fear that you have about the situation now. Also ask yourself what feelings you have about attempting to repair the damage.

**Intentions you now have.** Perhaps the most difficult part is to determine what you hope to accomplish by doing some repair work. Sometimes our intentions are not helpful. If, for example, your intent is to look good to others, you probably need to take a longer look at your motives.

**Amends you can make for the harm caused.** Name specific actions that will make up for what happened. Sometimes that may mean simply saying "I'm sorry." You will find some situations for which nothing can be done. For example, you have no idea how to reach someone, and the only amend you can make is to live your life differently. In some situations, further contact might cause further harm. At least you will be able to integrate that fact into your self-awareness. At the conclusion, you will have a list of all the amends you are willing to make. You will also have some blank spaces when it comes to amends.

As you can see, this will be a lengthy, difficult, soul-searching process that requires creativity and courage. Your guides can be important here. By reviewing your process as you go along, your guides can help you stay in reality. Their reactions to certain events may differ from yours, or they may challenge your intentions or suggest alternative actions. Remember, these amends do not have to be done all at once. You deserve time to think and to feel as you work through the process. Again, gentleness is your goal.

The next several pages provide a worksheet for you to use. At the bottom of each list is a space labeled "Date." As you make each amend, record the date it was completed. By updating the column, you will know exactly where you are on your Ninth Step. Entering the dates will remind you to call your guides and update them as well.

# Record of Those Harmed and Amends Made

**Person:** _____

_____

Memories of harm: _____

_____

_____

_____

_____

Thoughts: _____

_____

Feelings: _____

_____

Intentions: _____

_____

Amends: _____

_____

**Date:** _____

# Record of Those Harmed and Amends Made

**Person:** _____

_____

Memories of harm: _____

_____

_____

_____

Thoughts: _____

_____

Feelings: _____

_____

Intentions: _____

_____

Amends: _____

_____

**Date:** _____

# Record of Those Harmed and Amends Made

**Person:** _____

_____

Memories of harm: _____

_____

_____

_____

_____

Thoughts: _____

_____

Feelings: _____

_____

Intentions: _____

_____

Amends: _____

_____

**Date:** _____

## Record of Those Harmed and Amends Made

**Person:** _____

_____

Memories of harm: _____

_____

_____

_____

_____

Thoughts: _____

_____

Feelings: _____

_____

Intentions: _____

_____

Amends: _____

_____

**Date:** _____

## Record of Those Harmed and Amends Made

**Person:** _____

_____

Memories of harm: _____

_____

_____

_____

_____

Thoughts: _____

_____

Feelings: _____

_____

Intentions: _____

_____

Amends: _____

_____

**Date:** _____

# The Healer Within

We all have untapped reserves of energy within us. We can learn to draw upon that strength. In non-Western cultures, the Healer is an integrating force in the life of its community and individuals. These Healers have several responsibilities, not just the healing of the sick. If we look at their responsibilities and then mirror them within ourselves, we may draw upon healing forces we did not know we possessed. We all have a Healer Within. We also have a Child Within that needs to be cared for, guided, and nurtured so that it can just be. Read the following descriptions of what Healers do, what your Healer Within does, and what your Child Within needs.

*What Healers do:*

Healers mobilize belief. They tap those sources of energy that have not been available to individuals by themselves.

> *What your Healer Within does:* It teaches you to trust your intuition and helps you believe in yourself.

> *What your Child Within does:* It preserves your sense of child-like innocence.

*What Healers do:*

Healers release energy. With enthusiasm or charisma they are a catalyst and motivating force.

> *What your Healer Within does:* It gathers energy that allows you to mobilize.

> *What your Child Within does:* It releases the energy in play.

*What Healers do:*

They make sense out of the chaos.

> *What your Healer Within does:* It protects you
> from the chaos by creating boundaries.

> *What your Child Within does:* It allows you to live
> in safety.

*What Healers do:*

Healers provide wisdom.

> *What your Healer Within does:* It accesses your
> own wisdom. Some ways to do this are journaling,
> meditating, and imaging solutions.

> *What your Child Within does:* It allows you to seek
> guidance.

*What Healers do:*

They convene community. They bind others in community
by uniting people with a feeling of belonging.

> *What your Healer Within does:* It gives you confidence
> to build community by organizing, participating, or
> reaching out.

> *What your Child Within does:* It affirms your need to
> belong to a community.

*What Healers do:*
Healers use symbols and metaphors to teach and help others understand.

> *What your Healer Within does:* It raises your awareness of symbols and metaphors and helps you make the connections and understand the analogies.

> *What your Child Within does:* It frees you to inherit the metaphors, symbols, and understanding.

*What Healers do:*
Healers are the storytellers. By preserving traditions, they anchor individuals in their community and place in history.

> *What your Healer Within does:* It acknowledges your story, your epoch, and your place in history.

> *What your Child Within does:* It gets to be the hero of the story.

*What Healers do:*
Healers provide care.

> *What your Healer Within does:* It nurtures the self.

> *What your Child Within does:* It accepts nurturing.

*What Healers do:*
Healers channel the spiritual.

> *What your Healer Within does:* It provides you access to the spiritual—the presence of God within.

> *What your Child Within does:* It grounds you to be present to the world and to emotions. Being present is a spiritual act.

*What Healers do:*

Healers lead the collective process.

> *What your Healer Within does:* It becomes a partner, a participant, in the process.

> *What your Child Within does:* It allows you to be vulnerable and to surrender to the process.

*What Healers do:*

Often Healers are wounded themselves. Healing their own brokenness gave them the wisdom to heal others.

> *What your Healer Within does:* It attends and heals your wounds and brokenness.

> *What your Child Within does:* It opens you to acknowledge suffering and admit pain.

*What Healers do:*

Healers witness the truth.

> *What your Healer Within does:* It discerns truth and recognizes falsehood for what it is.

> *What your Child Within does:* It speaks and lives the truth.

When we call upon the Healer Within, we have a powerful resource for healing our Child Within. The Healer Within becomes a protector and champion to our Child Within. It allows the Child Within to preserve its innocence. It allows it to play, feel safe, seek guidance, and accept the desire to belong to its community. The Child Within inherits the heroic epics, stories, and metaphors that interpret inner chaos and provide wisdom. The Healer Within allows the Child to trust in its own spirituality by being present to the world, acknowledging suffering and pain, and speaking the truth. The Healer Within allows the Child Within to accept nurturing and not fear being vulnerable.

# Meditation

The following meditation is designed to help you visualize your Healer Within for the Child Within. You may choose to make a voice recording of yourself reading it and then play it back, or have someone read it aloud to you. Pause for ten to fifteen seconds where indicated, or stop the recording, before continuing.

*Find a nice, comfortable position.*

*If you are feeling anything emotionally distressing, picture yourself putting it in a box and setting it aside until the meditation is over. [pause]*

*Get in touch with your own bodily rhythms, your breathing, your heart rate. With each breath you take, each beat of your heart, you are participating in the larger rhythms of the universe. Each of those beats, each of those rhythms, has a sacredness to it because it is part of the forces of the universe. [pause]*

*Imagine that you are lying in a meadow on a summer day. You can feel the sun on your body. You feel very, very peaceful. You can hear the birds singing, smell the flowers and the grasses of the field. [pause]*

*You feel beckoned, as if you are being asked to go somewhere. You hear a voice calling you. You gently sit up. You look around. At the end of the meadow is a road. You know that road is where you need to go. You get up and walk to the road at the edge of the meadow. You walk down the road. As you walk, you come around the corner to a lake where there is a beach. There a child is playing in the sand on the beach. [pause]*

*As you approach, you see something familiar about that child. You leave the road. As you come closer, you see that the child is you at the age of five. This is what you looked like. This is who you were at the age of five. You get down on your knees and look at the child at the child's level, and you ask the child how the child is doing.*

*What does the child say to you? [pause]*

*Walk with the child. Invite the child to come along with you on your journey. Reach out and offer the child your hand. Ask the child to join you. The two of you leave the beach and go on down the road. [pause]*

*As you walk down the road, you come to some large hills at the base of a mountain. Up on one of the hills is a large, sanctuary-like building. You and the child approach the building. There is a long flight of stairs in front of the building. As the two of you come to the flight of stairs, a man and a woman walk out. They are so peaceful looking. They say, "Come, we have been waiting for you." You and the child walk up the stairs, and the man and the woman each take your hands and say, "We're so glad you are here."*

*Now they invite you in. They say to you, "We want to take you to what we call the room of vision." They guide you into a room with multicolored glass in the ceiling and skylights. There is no furniture, but a soft, spongy floor and four walls. [pause]*

*Your guides ask you to sit down. They explain to you that the room of visions is a way to have windows into your life.*

*The woman guide turns to your child and asks, "What is hurting you?" [pause] "How do you hurt right now?" [pause] What does your child say to the woman right now? [pause] The man turns to you and asks, "What is troubling you?" [pause] What do you say to the man? [pause]*

Then the woman explains, "We brought you here because we know you are troubled and we believe that there are things you already know that can help. Each wall to this room contains a vision. Two of the walls have visions of your possible futures. These are not the only possibilities. In each case, though, you will need to choose whether it is a future you want. Let's look at the first one."

The wall dissolves and there is an image of your future. You are watching you in your own future. What is this image about? [pause] What is happening in your future? [pause] What do you see? [pause] How do you react to this vision of the future? [pause] Look at your child. How is your child reacting to this vision from the future? [pause] The man says to you, "Now, remember, you can choose whether you want this in your future. Make a decision."

Look at your child. Is the child comfortable? [pause] Look at the future. Do you want this as part of your future? [pause] Make your decision and, as you decide, watch as the wall goes blank.

The guides then point to another wall. It dissolves and another vision comes out of your future. What is happening in this vision? [pause] What are you doing? [pause] Who are you with? [pause] How does it look like you are feeling in this future? [pause] How do you feel watching it? [pause] How does your child feel? [pause] Look at your child. How is your child reacting to it? [pause]

The woman says to you, "Now, again you can make a decision. Is this what you want?" [pause] "Is this what you want in your future?" [pause] "Choose." As you make your decision, the wall becomes opaque again. [pause]

The man guide says, "Behind the third wall are gifts. The child is to go first." The wall dissolves, and there is a gift waiting there for the child. What is the gift? [pause] "This is a spiritual gift," the man says. "Have your child go and get the gift and then come back and sit down on the soft, warm floor."

As you look up, your other guide says, "There is a gift in there for you, a spiritual gift. Let it be a symbol for you." What is the gift? [pause] What does it look like? [pause] What characteristics does it have? [pause] Get up and walk over to the gift. Pick it up and bring it back.

Behind the fourth wall, your guide says, "Picture an animal that you think is like you. An animal that can have special significance." Your child goes first. What animal appears for your child? [pause] Your guide asks, "How are you like this animal?" [pause] "In what ways are you like this animal?" [pause]

Now it is your turn. What animal fits for you? [pause] The wall dissolves and you can picture that animal. What is it like? [pause] How are you like that animal? [pause] What characteristics does it have that are like you? [pause]

Your guide says, "Let these animals serve as symbols for you of what you are about. Learn about them. Study them. They will teach you what you need to know."

You and your guides rise and you walk out of the building, into a garden, and down the stairs. You sit down next to your child. Spend a little time now, talking to that child. What do the Healers say to that child? [pause] What did you learn? [pause] How can you use the gifts? [pause] What about the future? Talk to the child, [pause]

As you finish the conversation, take the child's hand and walk back to the beach.

*Promise your child that you will let your child play, but that you will leave now. Whenever that child needs you, you will be back. Promise that the Healer Within you will always be there for the child. [pause]*

*As you walk away, back toward the meadow, you are aware that something has shifted. Something will never be the same. You feel steadier. You trust yourself. You are more peaceful. As you lay down in the meadow, you can feel the presence of the moment, how you blend into the earth, embracing it. You decide to rest, and you go to sleep.*

*When you are ready to finish the fantasy, awake and arise slowly and peacefully. Hold onto the feelings of your imagery.*

Healing is a matter of nurture, comfort, story, images, and personal connection. There are times when the child needs the healer, but there are also times when the healer needs the playfulness of the child. Metaphors are another way to get at your reality. If someone told you to play more, that you have the capability, it wouldn't be very effective. But if you can image yourself as an animal playing, or the child playing, it becomes believable to you on a conscious level. The visualization you just completed is a metaphor.

Describe your images and thoughts during the process.

_____

_____

_____

_____

_____

_____

_____

_____

_____

_____

_____

_____

_____

_____

# Affirmations

Affirmations can help us change our behavior. We can replace unhealthy messages that we did not choose with healthy messages we select. Each affirmation is written in the present—as if you are already accomplishing it. Even though it may not be a reality for you today, you need to "act as if." It may be difficult, but think of it as planting a garden with possibilities that will bloom with wonderful realities.

Select from the list the affirmations that have meaning for you, and add some of your own. Read them each day or as you need them.

- *I take responsibility for my part in my interpersonal relationships.*

- *I am ruthlessly honest in determining my part in a relationship that has been damaged.*

- *I can restore my own integrity by being willing to change, to disclose secrets, create new boundaries, be discerning in understanding systems, be willing to finish things, be open to new relationships and take responsibility.*

- *I am willing to look honestly at my sexual relationships. I acknowledge that as a sexual being, my sexuality is an integral part of my recovery. I apply honesty and spirituality to healing the sexual part of my life.*

- *I am open to the spiritual healing of the amends process. Whatever the outcome of my attempt, I will take pride in trying to make my amend.*

- *I ask for guidance in choosing whether to make an amend. With this guidance, I will not hurt myself or anyone further.*

- *I am open to the lessons that I can learn from making amends, and I am grateful for them.*

Create additional affirmations that are meaningful to you:

_____

_____

_____

_____

_____

_____

_____

_____

_____

_____

_____

_____

_____

_____

_____

## Reflections on the Eighth and Ninth Steps

If we are painstaking about this phase of our development, we are halfway through. We are going to know a new freedom and a new happiness. We will not regret the past or wish to shut the door on it. We will comprehend the word serenity and we will know peace. No matter how far down the scale we have gone, we will see how our experience can benefit others. That feeling of uselessness and self-pity will disappear. We will lose interest in selfish things and gain interest in our fellows. Self-seeking will slip away. Our whole attitude and outlook upon life will change. Fear of people and of economic insecurity will leave us. We will intuitively know how to handle situations that used to baffle us. We will suddenly realize that God is doing for us what we could not do for ourselves.

— *Alcoholics Anonymous*, the "Big Book"

These are the famous promises of the program. Reflect on completing your Eighth and Ninth Steps.

_____

_____

_____

_____

_____

_____

_____

_____

_____

Guides: What examples of the promises at work do you see in the life of this workbook owner?

Record your reactions.

_____

_____

_____

_____

_____

_____

_____

_____

_____

_____

_____

_____

_____

_____

_____

_____

Guide name: _____

Date: _____

The Eighth and Ninth Steps apply the Serenity Prayer to our relationships. They require us to identify the people we have harmed, to have difficult conversations with them, and then, as best we can, to change our relationships with them in positive ways. Steps Eight and Nine also require us to acknowledge and let go of what is unchangeable in our relationships with these people. As a result, these Steps help us put an end to many of the worries that have eaten away at us.

Working the Eighth and Ninth Steps means feeling and accepting our own pain about what we did in the past. We need to admit to ourselves that we hurt people, and we will likely feel sadness, grief, and healthy guilt. As we feel and process these emotions, we can then move through and out of them.

Having difficult conversations with people we harmed expands our awareness and helps us see that the story we told ourselves in relation to them may not be true or accurate. When we let someone else tell us their story about what we did and what effect it had on them—and when we really listen to what they say—we internally experience what they experienced. We may also begin to rewrite our own internal story of what happened. All of this changes our brain in many positive ways. As we put ourselves in the position of what it was like to be on the receiving end of our actions, we grow our mirror neuron system. This helps our brain relearn empathy and compassion. It improves our ability to solve problems. It also makes us more able to have empathy for ourselves.

In working Steps Eight and Nine, we need to say to people, "I'm sorry; I made mistakes; how can I make amends?" and then we need to make what amends we can. This creates closure, which in turn creates other positive changes in our brain. We can finally let go, because there's nothing about the relationship to worry about or obsess over anymore. We've removed the problem from our mental plate. This frees up mental and emotional bandwidth that we can make available to other people and concerns. This clearing out and letting go can help us be more present, as well. We may also feel profound relief and a great sense of lightness.

# Step Ten

*Continued to take personal inventory and
when we were wrong promptly admitted it.*

STEP TEN ASKS YOU to integrate the program principles of
honesty and spiritual exploration into your daily life. By now you
will have noticed that the program asks you at different points to
be a list maker. Making lists becomes one way for you to develop
personal awareness. Daily monitoring of the realities of your
strengths and limitations plus a willingness to acknowledge your
failings and successes is the surest path to sanity. From the beginning of this workbook we have emphasized balance, focus, and self-
responsibility. Applying those concepts to Step Ten, we see:

**Balance**—acknowledging strengths and limitations

**Focus**—taking a daily personal inventory

**Self-responsibility**—acknowledging successes and
failures promptly

This commitment to integrity lays the foundation for active
spirituality. Conversely, such rigorous ongoing self-examination can
be sustained only with a strong spiritual base—Step Eleven. The
combination of the two becomes a way of life for program people.
The spiritual component grows through daily readings, meditation,
prayer, and journal writing.

## Impact of Recovery Activities

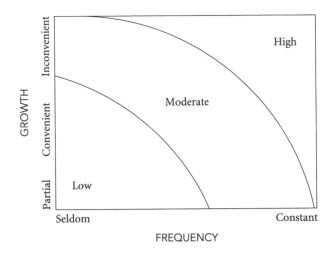

By maintaining this balance, focus, and self-responsibility, recovering people create an open system that grows and adapts. This contrasts with the closed (rigid, judgmental) and the chaotic (random, purposeless) systems of addiction and coaddiction. Making lists, doing Step work, keeping a journal, attending workshops, and participating in therapy and treatment are all examples of recovery activities that help expand our awareness and growth. A growing system stays in balance.

### Partial, Convenient, and Inconvenient Recovery

Simply going through the Twelve Steps once is not a solution. Working the Steps is an ongoing commitment—and recovery is something we never complete. As Step Ten teaches us, it's an unending process, a way of life.

In recovery, we revisit the Steps over and over. Sometimes we go through all the Steps in sequence. Sometimes we have to stop and revisit one Step in particular. Each time we revisit a Step, however, it's a different experience, because *we* are different.

As the diagram on the previous page suggests, there are three types of recovery: partial, convenient, and inconvenient. Let's look carefully at each one.

We've achieved *partial recovery* when we no longer practice our addictive or compulsive behavior. We're not in crisis right now, and the drama of addiction has subsided. We've gotten help from a Twelve Step group, and perhaps from a counselor or doctor or mental health practitioner. It's a good start—but it's only a start. In partial recovery, we've grown a helpful protective scab over our wound of addiction. But the wound is not fully healed.

If we imagine that the Twelve Steps are medicine, and that now we're cured and don't need them anymore, we're stuck in stinking thinking—and we're setting up ourselves for relapse. We don't understand that the Twelve Steps are food rather than medicine. We need them regularly, not just when we hurt.

People in partial recovery often take from the program but don't give back. They don't help other people, don't become sponsors, and don't volunteer to serve their Twelve Step groups. When they see other people in trouble, they lack the wisdom to think, *There but for the grace of God go I.*

If we stick with the process of recovery and continue to work the Steps, we eventually reach the stage of *convenient recovery*. At this point, we've seen many positive things take place in our life, so we're glad we hung in with recovery—but we're also keenly aware of how much time, effort, soul-searching, and painful feelings have been involved. We willingly help other people in recovery; perhaps we serve as a sponsor and volunteer in our Twelve Step group. But we still hope for an eventual end to the process and pain of recovery. We may say to ourselves, "Recovery is inconvenient and uncomfortable. When do I get to stop?"

We never get to stop, of course. Life never stops presenting us with difficult issues, so we'll never reach a point where we don't need the Twelve Steps anymore. We'll never stop rewriting our story, either, and we'll often need to revisit issues we've dealt with many times before.

One hallmark of people who are caught in convenient recovery is their hesitancy to stand up and be counted. They often haven't told their story of addiction in front of a group. They don't realize that part of healing any addiction or compulsion is talking about their experience before a group of people who care and understand.

Then there is *inconvenient recovery*—what some people might call "full recovery" or "real recovery." We are in inconvenient recovery when we no longer look for a way out, a way to declare the process complete. We understand that life will always require us to change, grow, and learn. We also understand that if we turn away from this demand, we begin to walk the path toward relapse. We recognize the need to continuously practice the principles of the Twelve Steps in all our affairs, to carry the message of recovery to all who wish to hear it, and to stay open to further spiritual awakenings. We realize that we are not in control of our life, and we regularly seek to carry out the will of our Higher Power. We let go of hoping that, somehow, some day, recovery and life will become comfortable and convenient.

# Balanced Equations:
# A Ten-Day Exercise for Steps Ten and Eleven

In the following exercise, ten equations are provided that represent the essential, but delicate, balance we all need in our lives. The first equation, the happiness equation, is taken from Dan Millman's *The Way of the Peaceful Warrior*, which served as the inspiration for the exercise. These equations are illustrations of the relative components of these key recovery issues.

| | |
|---|---|
| Happiness | Achievement |
| Growth | Intimacy |
| Serenity | Productivity |
| Peace of mind | Health |
| Reality | Spirituality |

Use each equation as a daily meditation upon imbalances in your life. Record your reflections, and then compose a prayer for each day, a prayer that helps you strike a balance. Stay in the moment. Describe thoughts and feelings that are present for you today.

At the end of the ten days, have a discussion with your guides about what process you would like to develop and use to maintain your conscious contact with God. Spirituality is fundamentally a personal and dynamic process. In addition to daily meditation and prayer, your plan to keep your connection to your Higher Power may include any practices—from helping others to sitting by a stream—that work for you. The exercises in the next section can help you achieve the balance you need to stay spiritually centered.

## Creating a Life of Congruence

In recovery, we work toward a life of congruence. When we live such a life, then what we say and what we do, the values we hold and the actions we take, the person others see and the person we experience ourselves to be, all match up.

Our life is simpler when it is congruent. We are not worried about being misunderstood, about being discovered, about people seeing through the lies we've told, or about keeping track of multiple stories. We are calm instead of anxious. We are most fully ourselves. We are also at our best.

The addict lives at least two lives at once, and often several. Invariably, these lives directly conflict with one another. When we live a life of congruence, however, all such conflicts automatically disappear.

The ten equations that follow are all about creating congruence and balance in your life. The left side of each equation always equals 1, or wholeness. Your task is to examine and modify your life so that the right side of each equation also equals 1.

As you may remember from taking math class years ago, any fraction that has the same number on top as on bottom equals 1. The fraction of 5 over 5 equals 1. The fraction of 10 over 10 equals 1. The fraction of 1 over 1 equals 1.

This means that the way to make each equation work—the way to help create the optimal happiness, growth, serenity, etc. in your life—is to equalize the two elements on the top and bottom of the fraction. When your desires and satisfaction are in balance, you'll experience optimal happiness. When the amount of change and the amount of stability in your life are roughly equivalent, that will yield optimal growth. And so it goes for each of the ten equations.

Working with these equations will help you uncover any incongruence in your life. For example, if you see that you spend almost all of your day doing things (for work, for family, for friends, as a volunteer, etc.) and almost none simply being (meditating, relaxing, being in nature, etc.), then this aspect of your life is out of balance, and your productivity is probably less than optimal. The equation reveals that this aspect of your life requires your attention in order to bring it into balance.

Now imagine that you spend most of your day in meditation and prayer, experiencing nature, and generally taking it easy. This same equation would reveal that your life is just as unbalanced, but in the other direction. You'll need to work toward bringing it back to balance and congruence.

The ten equations are a simple way to make a personal inventory. They will identify which aspects of your life need tweaking or re-engineering. Ultimately, they will help you live a spiritual life. The ten equations are spread out over ten days, one per day in the following exercises, but you can do these at a pace and in the order that suits your needs. Write a reflection and prayer that helps you bring each equation into balance.

# Day One:
## Happiness = Satisfaction/Desires

Happiness exists when what you want is matched by what you have. If your desires are few, they are easy to satisfy.

Are you so obsessed with what you do not have that you miss what you have now? Are your desires so intense that you always have to be striving for more to satisfy them?

**Reflection**

_____

_____

_____

_____

_____

_____

_____

_____

_____

_____

_____

_____

_____

_____

_____

**Prayer**

_____

_____

_____

_____

_____

_____

_____

_____

_____

_____

_____

_____

_____

_____

_____

_____

_____

_____

_____

_____

_____

_____

# Day Two:
## Growth = Change/Stability

Systems need to change or they die. Change is an essential ingredient to growth. Change without a stable foundation, however, leads to chaos. Any recovery program has elements of change as well as elements of stability.

Do you have a stable foundation to support your growth? Are you afraid to risk change, remaining stuck where you are?

**Reflection**

_____

_____

_____

_____

_____

_____

_____

_____

_____

_____

_____

_____

_____

**Prayer**

_____

_____

_____

_____

_____

_____

_____

_____

_____

_____

_____

_____

_____

_____

_____

_____

_____

_____

_____

_____

_____

_____

# Day Three:
## Serenity = Boundaries/Options

Addicts and coaddicts live in the extremes, which means they can take any option to an excess. Imposing limits in the form of boundaries creates balance. The Serenity Prayer epitomizes this principle by praying for courage "to change the things I can."

Do you pursue all your possibilities without any limits? Are you too caring, too helpful, too involved, too committed, too generous? Do you try to change things you can't? Looking at your own recent experience, how accurate have you been at discerning what you can and cannot change?

**Reflection**

_____

_____

_____

_____

_____

_____

_____

_____

_____

_____

_____

_____

**Prayer**

_____

_____

_____

_____

_____

_____

_____

_____

_____

_____

_____

_____

_____

_____

_____

_____

_____

_____

_____

_____

_____

# Day Four:
## Peace of Mind = Known to Others/Known to Self

Anxiety originates in secrets about yourself that others do not know. Worry about others discovering the truth destroys your peace of mind. When there are others in your life who know all there is to know, you can be peaceful and stop living in terror of another abandonment.

Are you living in fear because of untold secrets? Have you lied to people because you wanted to avoid conflict or hurting someone? Do you have friends you can confide your fear to?

**Reflection**

_____

_____

_____

_____

_____

_____

_____

_____

_____

_____

_____

_____

# Prayer

_____

_____

_____

_____

_____

_____

_____

_____

_____

_____

_____

_____

_____

_____

_____

_____

_____

_____

_____

_____

_____

_____

_____

# Day Five:
## Reality = Light Side/Dark Side

Reality includes acknowledging both your strengths and your weaknesses. To focus only on your failures distorts reality. To see only the successes equally blurs your vision. Both need to be fully—not partially—acknowledged and accepted.

Your light side contains your strengths, your abilities, your achievements, and your positive impact on the world. Your dark side includes your weaknesses, your areas of limited knowledge and ability, and your hot buttons. It also includes thoughts, habits, or impulses that you know are unhealthy or unfair. These might be things such as smoking, driving too fast, not being honest on your taxes, or sometimes snapping at your partner.

Do you have more difficulty admitting strengths or weaknesses? Do you fully admit that you have both? Are there particular ones that you have trouble acknowledging?

**Reflection**

_____

_____

_____

_____

_____

_____

_____

_____

_____

# Prayer

_____

_____

_____

_____

_____

_____

_____

_____

_____

_____

_____

_____

_____

_____

_____

_____

_____

_____

_____

_____

_____

_____

_____

# Day Six:
# Achievement = Vision/Plan

Genuine achievement combines both an image of what needs to be done and a concrete plan of action to get the tasks done. A plan without vision goes unfulfilled, either falling apart or slipping off course. A vision without concrete action never becomes reality. Part of thinking a day at a time is to break a dream down into little pieces that can be done a piece at a time. Achievement often means facing your fears about what you feel called to do, and moving forward in spite of them.

Do you procrastinate about taking action on your ideas? Do you think about what you want to do before you act? Do you break big dreams into daily, doable pieces?

**Reflection**

_____

_____

_____

_____

_____

_____

_____

_____

_____

_____

_____

**Prayer**

_____

_____

_____

_____

_____

_____

_____

_____

_____

_____

_____

_____

_____

_____

_____

_____

_____

_____

_____

_____

_____

_____

# Day Seven:
## Intimacy = Fidelity to Self/Fidelity to Others

Ultimately, intimacy exists because of trust. When fidelity to yourself matches faithfulness to others, trust occurs. People who report clearly their own needs, boundaries, and feelings are trustworthy. You can predict—or trust—what they will do. If you are accountable to others, people will feel safe being close to you.

Do you compromise yourself or give in too easily and then get mad? Do you say yes when you really want to say no? Do you follow through on your promises? Can people trust you enough to be intimate?

**Reflection**

_____

_____

_____

_____

_____

_____

_____

_____

_____

_____

_____

**Prayer**

_____

_____

_____

_____

_____

_____

_____

_____

_____

_____

_____

_____

_____

_____

_____

_____

_____

_____

_____

# Day Eight:
# Productivity = Being/Doing

Truly productive people take time to recreate themselves by doing nothing. Stopping to enjoy all that is around you is essential to renewing your energy. What you do needs to be matched by times of simply being.

Do you stop to smell the flowers? Do you have busy vacations? Do you have daily down time? Do you take time to be quiet? Are you meditating too much and not accomplishing anything concrete?

**Reflection**

_____

_____

_____

_____

_____

_____

_____

_____

_____

_____

_____

_____

_____

# Prayer

_____

_____

_____

_____

_____

_____

_____

_____

_____

_____

_____

_____

_____

_____

_____

_____

_____

_____

_____

_____

# Day Nine:
# Health = Awareness/Practice

As a recovering person, you need to take greater responsibility for your health. This means that you need to learn about it and develop your awareness. Your awareness must be matched by action. Do you do what you know you should?

Are there aspects of your own health you need to know more about? Do you take care of yourself physically and respect your body? Are you doing what you need to?

**Reflection**

_____

_____

_____

_____

_____

_____

_____

_____

_____

_____

_____

_____

_____

_____

# Prayer

_____

_____

_____

_____

_____

_____

_____

_____

_____

_____

_____

_____

_____

_____

_____

_____

_____

_____

_____

_____

_____

_____

# Day Ten:
## Spirituality = Mortality/Meaning

Spirituality starts with understanding your own human limitations, beginning with your mortality. Given those limits, you need to explore what meaning they have for you. Philosophical speculation without the reality of your human limits has no foundation and quickly becomes irrelevant. Daily life becomes pointless and without a sense of higher purpose.

Do you live each day as if it were your last? Did you find time today to address your priorities?

**Reflection**

_____

_____

_____

_____

_____

_____

_____

_____

_____

_____

_____

_____

_____

# Prayer

_____

_____

_____

_____

_____

_____

_____

_____

_____

_____

_____

_____

_____

_____

_____

_____

_____

_____

_____

_____

_____

_____

## Daily Tenth Step Inventory

Using the equations as reminders, each day mentally review these areas of your life as a Tenth Step inventory.

| | |
|---|---|
| **Happiness** | Did you balance satisfaction with desires? |
| **Growth** | Did you balance your need for stability with what is healthy, new, and different? |
| **Serenity** | Did you balance your possibilities with your limitations? |
| **Peace of Mind** | Did you take the risk to not keep secrets from those you trust? |
| **Reality** | Can you acknowledge the strengths and weaknesses that you demonstrated today? |
| **Achievement** | Did you act on your plan and your vision for yourself today? |
| **Intimacy** | Did you find balance between your boundaries and accountability to others? |
| **Productivity** | Was there balance between what you accomplished and moments of peace for you today? |
| **Health** | What did you do today to take care of your body? |
| **Spirituality** | What action did you take today to touch your higher purpose and your own humanity? |

## Affirmations

Affirmations help us change our behavior. Make a recording of yourself reading the following affirmations aloud. Then play it back and listen to the person you are becoming. Pause a few seconds after each affirmation.

- *I create my own happiness by allocating my resources to achieve those things that give me satisfaction.*

- *I have a firm foundation of stability in several areas of my life that allows me to positively change to continue my growth in recovery.*

- *The options I select and the boundaries I establish give me serenity.*

- *My peace of mind comes from trusting my intimate circle with my reality.*

- *I accept my strengths and weaknesses, my good and bad choices that help me through the gray of reality.*

- *Vision creates the purpose and direction for my life. I achieve my purpose with planning and execution—one piece at a time.*

- *Trust in myself and in others allows me intimacy.*

- *My productivity is maximized when I accomplish tasks and spend time recreating myself.*

- *I perform healthful practices out of respect and reverence for my body's needs.*

- *Each moment in my day holds an opportunity to give my life higher meaning by how I choose to live it.*

Create additional affirmations that are meaningful to you:

_____

_____

_____

_____

_____

_____

_____

_____

_____

_____

_____

_____

_____

_____

_____

_____

_____

_____

## Reflections on the Tenth Step

We must always hold truth, as best we can determine it, to be more important, more vital to our self-interest, than our comfort. Conversely, we must always consider our personal discomfort relatively unimportant and, indeed, even welcome it in the service or the search for truth. Mental health is an ongoing process of dedication to reality at all costs . . . What does a life of total dedication to truth mean? It means, first of all, a life of continuous and never ending stringent self-examination.

— M. Scott Peck, M.D.
*The Road Less Traveled*

Reflect on the words of Scott Peck and think of your daily meditation and prayer practices. Do they help you maintain conscious contact with your Higher Power? Do they help you with your ongoing personal inventory?

_____

_____

_____

_____

_____

_____

_____

_____

_____

_____

Guides: What do you see happening on a daily basis in the life of this workbook owner?

Share your insights, feelings, and suggestions.

_____

_____

_____

_____

_____

_____

_____

_____

_____

_____

_____

Guide name: _____

Date: _____

# Step Eleven

*Sought through prayer and meditation to improve our conscious contact with* God *as we understood Him,* praying only for knowledge of His will for us and the power to carry that out.

SPIRITUAL RENEWAL has many forms. Throughout this book we have suggested a variety of strategies and activities. Those suggestions certainly fit the intention of Step Eleven. Sometimes we need to make an extraordinary effort, especially if we are in need of direction in our lives. Spirituality is simply another level of knowing or finding. Often this takes the form of a journey or quest. To undertake such a spiritual quest, you will need to make special preparations. Following are suggestions for what you might need.

**A dream journal.** Buy yourself a book with blank pages. As you plan and prepare for this quest, keep a log of all dreams you remember, even if they are only fragments. If you have trouble remembering your dreams, keep a recording device by your bed. Transcribe the dreams in the morning. Record the day, the dream, and the feelings you had as part of the dream. Dreams bear important messages from within ourselves. While on your quest, your dream log may become very important to you.

**A seeking place.** Select a time when you will be undisturbed, such as during a weekend, series of weekends, week, month—whatever you can manage to dedicate to your spiritual quest. This time should be when you can lay daily demands aside and not be distracted by family, friends, job, or other factors.

**A guiding metaphor.** Look for an analogy, metaphor, image, or icon for this time of your life. Survivors of child abuse, for example, often use the turtle. They notice how the ways of the turtle can be helpful. Turtles are survivors of eons of evolution. They evolved a tough shell to protect vulnerable parts. They pursue a deliberate pace on land but allow themselves grace in the open seas. And they know how to pull in to avoid harm. Find a metaphor, analogy, image, or icon that can help you think about this time.

For example, I often use a turtle as a metaphor for many aspects of recovery, because a turtle takes life one step at a time. It focuses on what's in front of it and has very good boundaries. It knows when to be out in the world and when to pull into its shell. For other aspects of recovery I use a hummingbird. It's the one creature that can see 360 degrees without turning its head. In recovery, we need to take the widest view possible, too. A hummingbird can also fly in any direction—and it can change direction quickly. So I frequently think of recovery as requiring us to see in all directions and to change and adapt quickly, like the hummingbird. But we also need the skills of the turtle, being able to protect ourselves and close our boundaries tight when we have to. Using their very different skills, both animals often travel thousands of miles.

**A collection of sacred things.** Native Americans have the concept of a medicine bundle. Recovering people use the concept of a "God box." Whatever term you use, gather together things of special significance to you that symbolize empowered moments of your life. Program medallions, sponsor gifts—collect anything that will help you connect with your own spiritual roots.

**A meditative practice.** All spiritual traditions provide exercises that have been proven to promote an inward calmness and stillness. Forms of meditation developed by science, such as Mindfulness-Based Stress Reduction, have proven equally helpful. A regular meditation practice can become the center of your spiritual life, and is all but indispensable to it. Such practices take many forms: silent sitting, silent walking, spiritual dancing, reciting prayers or mantras, chanting, following your breath, or focusing on an image. All these forms of meditation dramatically improve the mind's ability to be present. They also help calm your mind so you can examine what it's doing and feeling. Feel free to experiment and find a meditative practice that feels comfortable and energizing to you.

**A spiritual mentor.** Based upon their own experience, a spiritual director or holy person can help you. Whether it be the exercises of St. Ignatius or the Vision Quest of the Sioux, holy persons help prepare you for the quest. They support you during the experience. They debrief you later to help you understand your experiences. They are special guides for this time.

Usually a quest takes months of preparation and lots of coaching from the spiritual mentor. Sometimes there are readings to be done, information to be gathered, or special materials to be found. There is no magic in this preparation. It is simply preparing yourself.

During the actual quest, take care to journal your experiences. Share them only with your spiritual guide. Allow time from daily living with your guide to process this retreat. We have included a planning sheet for you to think about your quest. We have provided space for your guide to memorialize whatever reactions he or she had.

Blessings on your effort!

## Spiritual Quest Planning Sheet

Complete the following in preparation for your quest.

1. What is the "seeking place" you will use?

_____

_____

2. When is your "seeking time"?

_____

_____

3. What metaphors, analogies, images, or icons will you use?

_____

_____

4. What special, sacred thing do you wish to bring with you?

_____

_____

5. Who will serve as your spiritual mentor?

_____

_____

6. What special instructions does your spiritual mentor suggest?

_____

_____

## Spiritual Quest Debriefing (for Spiritual Guides)

This sheet is intended for spiritual guides to share their reactions and observations with those they have supported in making a spiritual quest. Write a letter affirming the quest and any special efforts and gains this person has made because of the experience. Summarize what learnings you see as most important for future action. Remember that this letter is a very important part of the workbook. It serves as a "meaning anchor" to deepen this person's spiritual experience and as a touchstone for the person's continuing journey in recovery.

Date: _____

Dear _____ ,

_____

_____

_____

_____

_____

_____

_____

_____

_____

_____

_____

_____

_____

_____

## Reflections on the Eleventh Step

Attending to our sorrow, queasy with bewilderment at whom we might be without, we must first cultivate mercy for ourselves, which will gradually expand into compassion for other sentient beings. We send wishes for the well-being of all who, like ourselves, share this same pain at this same moment and who also wish only to be free. Using the mirror of compassionate mindfulness, we recognize our reflection amongst the throngs of sentient beings to whom the true heart, the healed heart, pledges service.

— Stephen Levine
*Unattended Sorrow*

Reflect on Stephen Levine's words and on your own Eleventh Step. How have you improved your conscious contact with your Higher Power? How has your life changed as a result of that contact? What has gotten in the way of such contact for you? How does the knowledge that all of us share the same pain, and the same desire for freedom, affect your relationship with your Higher Power?

# Step Twelve

*Having had a spiritual awakening as the result of
these steps, we tried to carry this message to alcoholics,
and to practice these principles in all our affairs.*

ONE OF THE MILLION reasons to do Twelve Step work is so you stay sober. But helping others is a significant part of the program, and there are many ways the program gets passed on. When you live the program and share it with others, you are carrying the message, especially when you sponsor new members. In practicing the Twelfth Step you will find that:

- Witnessing to others, your appreciation of the program and the program's impact on your life deepens.

- Hearing the stories of new members, you are reminded of where you were when you started.

- Modeling to others, you become aware that you need to practice what you preach.

- Giving to others, you develop bonds with new people who really need you.

- Helping others, you give what you have received.

- Supporting new beginnings, you revitalize your own efforts.

Being a sponsor sounds intimidating, but there are only a few things you need to do:

- Work hard to understand the whole story of the person you are sponsoring.

- Give emotional support to the person during those difficult times.

- Help the person to focus on the basics of your particular program.

- Help the person to focus on the Steps of the program.

As you deepen your relationships with those you sponsor, you will find good things about them that they overlook. (Remember when all you could find to report to your sponsor was the latest disaster?) You will work hard to help new members see what they are doing right. Addicts and coaddicts, by definition, see only the bad in themselves. Perhaps the most priceless gifts a sponsor can give are those beginning affirmations.

As a sponsor, you serve as a special role model. How you work your program will have a significant impact on those you help. To bolster your confidence, have your guides share their reactions to your being a sponsor using the space provided.

You also need to be very clear about your own definition of sobriety. To review that again will help you be more clear with the person you are sponsoring. No doubt your understanding of your sobriety has evolved since those early days when you told the group what you would not do. The sobriety worksheet provided reflects the old Buddhist axiom that wisdom is being able to say yes as well as no. In sobriety terms, this means that recovery is more than abstinence from self-destructive behavior. It is also a positive statement about what you embrace. Much of this has probably been clear to you for some time, but recording and discussing your personal standards of sobriety with your own guides will be helpful to you and those you are about to help.

Remember, your path is gentle. You can get help in learning to help others. Your Higher Power will be with you.

# Twelfth Step Guide Affirmations

The purpose of this page is for your guides to affirm you and your suitability to help others on the gentle path.

Please show this book to several trusted friends and guides. Ask each one to write down one to several sentences that describe your talents, abilities, and strengths. Each of these messages can serve as an affirmation, and a source of inspiration, as you continue to walk the gentle path.

Note to guides and friends: As you list affirmations, the more specific you can be, the more helpful the affirmations will be.

*Example:* You are one of the best listeners I know. —S.K.

1. _____

   _____

2. _____

   _____

3. _____

   _____

4. _____

   _____

5. _____

   _____

6. _____

_____

7. _____

_____

8. _____

_____

9. _____

_____

10. _____

_____

11. _____

_____

12. _____

_____

13. _____

_____

14. _____

_____

15. _____

_____

## Sobriety Worksheet

Now that you have come this far along the gentle path, it's time to create a sobriety worksheet to keep your recovery on course. This worksheet will be an exceptionally valuable tool to use as a reference guide in the weeks and months to come. Review it regularly.

Here are the basic directions with some very simple examples.

1. Specify a list of concrete sobriety boundaries in the space below. *Example: No use of alcohol or other drugs.*

2. List specific behaviors that could jeopardize or endanger your ability to preserve your boundary. *Example: Boundaries—Drinking any alcohol. Smoking pot. Danger Zones—Getting too hungry, angry, lonely, or tired. Talking to my parents about certain touchy subjects.*

3. Take each sobriety boundary and complete a sobriety worksheet for each one. Start by entering the boundary on the designated line. Record the last date of that behavior on the sobriety date line. *Example: Drinking alcohol. February 2, 2012.*

4. For each individual boundary, record the actual behaviors that would constitute a slip and require a revision of your sobriety date. Focus on those specific behaviors that were part of your addictive life. Record on the line labeled "Behaviors That Equal a Slip." *Example: Drinking beer at my favorite bar.*

5. Next, list the behaviors that are not actual slips, but would detract from, or endanger, your sobriety. These are the behaviors that usually occurred before the actual addictive behavior. In other words, these are the things you usually did before a certain acting out or binge. Realizing this, you also know that these are potentially seductive behaviors and can lead you into a real danger zone. Record on the line labeled "Behaviors That Endanger Sobriety Boundary." *Example: Going to my favorite bar, but not drinking beer.*

6. Fantasy is an integral part of the addictive experience. Whether excessive daydreaming, fantasizing, or actual trancelike preoccupations, these mental states are conducive to engaging in the old bad habits. Remembering that you alone know your obsessive thoughts and that only you are responsible for protecting your sobriety, list those fantasies that are unhealthy for you. Record on the line labeled "Fantasy." *Example: Reminiscing about good times and good beer at my favorite bar.*

7. Finally, record those positive actions you now know will affirm or strengthen your sobriety boundaries. These behaviors will serve as survival action steps to help you through the difficult times that are bound to come on the path to sobriety and serenity. Don't forget to state what you will work for. Record on the line labeled "Action Step to Strengthen, Affirm Sobriety." *Example: When I begin thinking about going to my favorite bar, I will call my sponsor. I will schedule regular activities with good friends who don't drink.*

**My Personal Sobriety Boundaries**

_____

_____

_____

_____

_____

_____

_____

_____

## Sobriety Worksheets

### Worksheet 1

---

| 1 |
| --- |

Sobriety Boundary

Sobriety Date

Behaviors that Equal a Slip

Behaviors that Endanger Sobriety

Fantasy

Action Step to Strengthen, Affirm Sobriety

---

### Worksheet 2

---

| 2 |
| --- |

Sobriety Boundary

Sobriety Date

Behaviors that Equal a Slip

Behaviors that Endanger Sobriety

Fantasy

Action Step to Strengthen, Affirm Sobriety

---

## Worksheet 3

3

Sobriety Boundary

Sobriety Date

Behaviors that Equal a Slip

Behaviors that Endanger Sobriety

Fantasy

Action Step to Strengthen, Affirm Sobriety

## Worksheet 4

4

Sobriety Boundary

Sobriety Date

Behaviors that Equal a Slip

Behaviors that Endanger Sobriety

Fantasy

Action Step to Strengthen, Affirm Sobriety

## Gifts of the Spirit

Sponsorship is only one of the ways Twelve Step work is done. One of the messages you carry in your journey is that of recovery. By your example, you will influence others, whether you intend to or not. If you have children, this is graphically clear. They rarely do what we say, but are sure to do what we do. Like snowflakes, we are all unique. Each of us possesses a unique combination of talents and inner strengths. We may not be aware of all of them just yet, but we are responsible for using them to the best of our ability. It is through these gifts that we can do our greatest Twelve Step work.

We all know people who allow us to feel emotions through their music, listeners who let us pour out our happiness or sadness and know how to make us feel cared for, those who have gifts of mathematical or scientific insight that help us make sense out of the unintelligible, wonderful cooks, great mechanics.... What are your gifts?

List your gifts of the spirit, your special talents and inner strengths.

(If you have trouble thinking of them, think of a time when you had great pleasure doing something. When someone said how meaningful or wonderful it was, you were surprised, maybe a little embarrassed. You had already received enjoyment for doing it and didn't expect others to enjoy it too.)

_____

_____

_____

_____

These gifts empower us. Perhaps within these gifts lies your vision, your mission. With the guidance of a Higher Consciousness, you can use them to make the dark places light.

## Beginning Again

Some things become obvious. By the third year of recovery, most of us learn to accept that boring is okay. One does not have to live in perpetual crisis. In the way we used to live, chaos was a way of life. Now we work to have reserves—emotional, financial, physical, and spiritual—so that when crises do occur, they do not throw us. We have the support we need.

However, it also becomes obvious that our lives are not problem-free. In fact, some of the old issues re-emerge again and again. The difference is that now we have the understanding and the skills to avoid old self-destructive patterns. Most of us sooner or later say to ourselves, "I'm tired of growing," or pray to God, "No more challenges, please!" So we search for balance between the forces in our lives, for stability and the forces for change.

Preserving that balance may bring us to a point where the program ceases to nurture us and becomes dry. How to generate new energy for program efforts is the challenge. Here are concrete actions you can take to revitalize your recovery.

### In Alliance with Others

**Do Service Work.** For many, the ticket for making progress in recovery has been participating in the fellowship and organizational life. Service in a group or intergroup alters your perceptions and expands awareness dramatically. Passing it on really does make a difference.

**Participate in National Events.** Most Twelve Step fellowships organize national conferences and retreats. For many, the effort it takes to participate is rewarded many times over. For some, attendance provides watershed-like experiences in their recovery.

**Participate in Group Retreats and Other Local Twelve Step Events.** Many Twelve Step meetings, districts, and areas sponsor retreats, picnics, seminars, roundups, conventions, and other events.

Participating in some of these is a great way to expand your relationships within the Twelve Step community and access wisdom about working a Twelve Step program.

**Ask for a Group Conscience Meeting.** It is traditional for each Twelve Step group to periodically inventory how well it is functioning. Such an inventory is an ideal opportunity to suggest and discuss changes. If your Twelve Step group is not holding group conscience meetings at least twice a year, think about asking for such a meeting. It could be a gateway to revitalizing group members' involvement— or to making the group more loving and effective.

**Join Another Program.** Most of us qualify to participate in another fellowship. An alcoholic, for example, has codependency issues and could dramatically change his or her life by attending Al-Anon. Resistance occurs because one does not want to be a beginner again. Joining another fellowship, for many, is exactly what is needed.

**Join a Couples Fellowship.** One of the most significant developments in the recovery groups has been the emergence of couples-oriented fellowships such as Recovering Couples Anonymous or Chapter Nine. Many have reported that joining such a fellowship with a life partner enhanced their recovery dramatically. Couples fellowships are built on the premise that when couples work the Twelve Steps together, each member of the couple experiences "your recovery, my recovery, and our recovery."

**Change Formats.** Many groups have found that changing formats can renew group life. Individuals also can shift focus. Join a write-and-share meeting or a spirituality-focused group.

**Tell Your Story to Someone New.** If you've had the same sponsor for a long time, perhaps now is a good time to find someone new— even if your current sponsor is a wise and wonderful person. This can create a helpful shift in your relationships within the program. A new sponsor may also have helpful insights and perspectives that your previous sponsor did not. Another option is to keep your original sponsor, but ask someone else to sponsor you as well. Many people in Twelve Step programs have more than one sponsor.

**On Your Own**

**Explore Your Resistance.** Sometimes we resist continuing our program efforts because if we continued to the next issue, it would be overwhelming. Sometimes the program becomes "dry" because we really do not want to deal with something. The question to ask is, what are we avoiding?

**Note Any Increases of Addictive Behavior.** Addiction can be cunning and baffling. Although we may no longer practice the addiction that brought us to the Twelve Steps, another addiction can slowly creep into our life, one day at a time, and take its place. Do you find yourself strongly drawn to a particular activity? Are you beginning to act compulsively with food, or sex, or gambling, or using the Internet? Have you taken up smoking, or do you smoke more than you used to?

**Look at the Larger Patterns in Your Life.** If you've lost some of your energy for recovery and the Twelve Steps, take time out to review your life as a whole. Is the energy loss strictly related to recovery, or do you feel your life in general is stuck or has gone dry? Either way, talk with your sponsor about how you feel. Consider what actions you can take to break (or shake up) the internal logjam in a healthy way.

**Lean Into Change.** Do you feel like you're coming up on a major shift in your life—or do you wish you were? Do you feel yourself resisting an upcoming change? Explore your feelings about the potential change, and talk with your sponsor about it.

**Revisit the Steps and Your Early Work with Them.** Reflect back on your experience with the Twelve Steps and how far you've come. Also recall the story you told when you first came into the program, and compare it with the story you tell now. As a result of this reflection, are there any Steps you would like to revisit and work anew?

## Reflections on the Twelfth Step

Denial is the hallmark of the immature, the insecure, the self-centered, the nonaffirmed. When Faust, the man who was willing to sell his soul to the devil and condemn himself to hell, asked his visitor who he was, Mephistopheles replied, "I am the spirit who always denies!"

— Conrad Baars
*Born Only Once*

The Twelfth Step requires that you share your path with others. The joy of your sobriety and its life-giving reality are what you have to give. Denial is how you have lost your way in the past. Reflect on the quote above and think about how the Twelfth Step can maintain reality in your life. Think, too, about the contract between the gift you offer new members and the offer of Mephistopheles. Record your reflections below.

_____

_____

_____

_____

_____

_____

_____

_____

_____

_____

The Tenth, Eleventh, and Twelfth Steps teach us that recovery is an ongoing process. When we work the Twelve Steps, we don't just use them as temporary tools; we make them a way of living.

This way of living involves ongoing reflection and improvement. It also involves passing on the wisdom of the Steps to others.

Through this focus on service—listening to others tell their stories, coaching them through a First Step, and helping them in other ways—we go back through the Steps ourselves. Each time we do, we encounter them with a new perspective and come away with new learnings.

The Twelve Steps also help us cultivate and strengthen a wise inner observer. You'll recall that this is the part of the brain that monitors all its internal traffic, all its different voices, and helps them work together in more effective ways. Over time, our brain starts to function at a higher level than it would have if we hadn't worked the Steps. One day at a time, our regrown brain creates not just health and sanity, but wisdom.

# Epilogue:
# Getting This Far

GETTING THIS FAR means you have worked very hard and have given many gifts to yourself. You have by now integrated Twelve Step principles into your core being, have changed your life dramatically, and have a rich community of friends. Let the workbook be a record of your transformation and a celebration of your courage.

There may come a time when you feel the need to revitalize your program. You may wish to complete the workbook again. People report that using these exercises at different times in their lives generated very different experiences. Feel free to repeat them. All you need is the desire, the courage, and some blank sheets of paper.

By now, you've probably realized that there is no finish line on the gentle path through the Twelve Steps. The Steps are a process—ongoing, regenerating, renewing. In recovery, as in life generally, there are always new challenges, and you will find, if you keep reaching out, plenty of friends along the way.

My congratulations! Welcome to the beginning of the rest of your journey.

— Patrick J. Carnes

# Appendix A

# The Twelve Traditions
## of Alcoholics Anonymous

### Tradition One

Our common welfare should come first; personal recovery depends upon A.A. unity.

### Tradition Two

For our group purpose there is but one ultimate authority—a loving God as He may express Himself in our group conscience. Our leaders are but trusted servants; they do not govern.

### Tradition Three

The only requirement for A.A. membership is a desire to stop drinking.

### Tradition Four

Each group should be autonomous except in matters affecting other groups or A.A. as a whole.

### Tradition Five

Each group has but one primary purpose—to carry its message to the alcoholic who still suffers.

### Tradition Six

An A.A. group ought never endorse, finance, or lend the A.A. name to any related facility or outside enterprise, lest problems of money, property, and prestige divert us from our primary purpose.

### Tradition Seven

Every A.A. group ought to be fully self-supporting, declining outside contributions.

### Tradition Eight

Alcoholics Anonymous should remain forever nonprofessional, but our service centers may employ special workers.

### Tradition Nine

A.A., as such, ought never be organized; but we may create service boards or committees directly responsible to those they serve.

### Tradition Ten

Alcoholics Anonymous has no opinion on outside issues; hence the A.A. name ought never be drawn into public controversy.

### Tradition Eleven

Our public relations policy is based on attraction rather than promotion; we need always maintain personal anonymity at the level of press, radio, and films.

### Tradition Twelve

Anonymity is the spiritual foundation of all our traditions, ever reminding us to place principles before personalities.

---

The Twelve Traditions are taken from *Twelve Steps and Twelve Traditions* (New York: Alcoholics Anonymous World Services, 1981), 129–87.

# Appendix B

# A Guide for Group Use

FROM THE BEGINNING, *A Gentle Path through the Twelve Steps* was meant to be an evolving resource for Twelve Step study. Over the past twenty-five years, groups all across the country have been using the workbook in different ways, with different goals, and with different stories to tell. We have put together some of their suggestions on what worked and what didn't work for them, and we have made some changes to the book based on their comments. Following are some of the ways *A Gentle Path through the Twelve Steps* can be used in a group setting.

- It can be an introduction to how the Twelve Steps work. With a guide or sponsor, this book can help you understand what the Twelve Steps mean in your life.

- As a study guide for renewal groups, the book has helped those in recovery reach deeper levels of understanding.

- For those with multiple or secondary addictions, it is a tool for exploring other sides of one's addictive self.

- The book can be used in therapy groups or with a therapist.

- It can be used simply as a resource for help in presentation of a Step talk, the same way the Twelve Steps and Twelve Traditions have been used for years.

The important component of group accountability will help you continue progressing through the book. It will be the support and encouragement of other members of the group that will get you through the difficult parts and hold you accountable to yourself in your goal of study and growth.

### Study Groups

Because every group brings its own expectations and experiences, each study group is unique. Following are some suggested variations.

**Post Meeting Mini-Group**. This is a smaller group that chooses to meet for an hour to an hour and a half after a main Twelve Step meeting. This has two distinct advantages. First, everyone in the group has already built a trust level from knowing each other in the main Twelve Step group. Second, it minimizes the nights away from spouses and the need for babysitters. By meeting in a smaller group, more in-depth work time can be spent on each individual.

**Write-and-Share Meeting.** In this format, one person writes a part of the assigned Step. At the meeting, this person shares what he or she has written, while the others in the group write their personal reflections on what the person has shared. Each member then takes a turn sharing reflections.

**Focus Group.** A focus group makes a commitment to use *A Gentle Path through the Twelve Steps* as a study guide. Group members commit a specific number of months that they plan to work on it. These groups require a sincere commitment on each member's part. To develop the trust level that is needed, the group should be closed, meaning no new members will come into the group after its formation. They operate basically as a write-and-share meeting. One group of four women in Michigan took only one to three pages each week, and with everyone sharing they found a connectedness in their experiences. Others' comments became catalysts to their own thoughts and feelings. A group of six men in Texas found that it worked better for them to have one person report each week on larger sections of the book. Each member was responsible for giving feedback to the person reporting. Without having to worry about what they were going to say when their turn came, they could give that person their full attention. These groups develop a deep sense of community.

**All-Day Self-Help Seminars.** A group may decide to use *A Gentle Path through the Twelve Steps* as the format for an all-day retreat or seminar. The format may have time for a presentation, time to use the workbook for the homework, and time for sharing.

### Variations

Individuals may choose to share the entire content of what they have written, or summarize their work if the group is particularly large.

It helps to bring in outside literature that pertains to the Step being worked on. We know of one group whose entire membership attended retreats and seminars that dealt with topics related to the Step they were working on.

Breaking bread together has always been a way of developing community. One group, determined not to get carried away, assigned a list of cold cuts, bread, condiments, chips, and refreshments and rotated who brought the ingredient for a sandwich meal every week. Another group confessed that it was comforting to have chocolate on the table when the Steps were really emotionally difficult. Some groups choose to go for coffee or lunch after meetings.

A group of young single parents pooled their money for one babysitter on Saturday mornings and brought their children with them to the church where they met. Their children had friends to play with while their parents worked the Step.

Groups with a diverse membership, or with members new to the Twelve Step program, may need greater structure in the meeting. Opening and closing rituals, like the Serenity Prayer or readings from various meditation books, can be familiar and comforting. A "check-in" time can be allowed at the beginning of each meeting, giving everyone a chance to say, in two or three sentences, how they are feeling or what is going on with them.

Because all addicts and coaddicts have trouble with intimacy, one group chose to practice being open to intimacy by holding the meetings in different group members' homes, rotating the site each month.

## Time Limits

How long will the group meet? One hour or more? It helps to have the members agree on the length of the meeting and how many weeks or months each member is willing to commit. In-depth renewal groups have taken up to two and a half years to complete the workbook. The group needs to re-examine its commitment from time to time, and recommit if necessary, to get the most out of the work.

The bonding that grows in *Gentle Path* study groups is very deep, but it can delay the start of the meeting. One group allows fifteen minutes for everyone's friendly greetings and conversation before they begin the meeting.

## Leadership

The group may choose to rotate leadership each week, month, or quarter. If only one person shares his or her work at a meeting, he or she may be the designated leader that week. The leadership method will vary with each group, but in the beginning it is important to have a group consensus. It may evolve and change without verbal discussion into what feels natural for the group. However, control can be abused or abdicated, so it is important to re-examine the group consensus from time to time.

## Feedback

A group in Colorado recommended to us that groups spend some time initially hashing out agreed-upon suggestions for feedback. By doing this, the group gets to understand individual sensitivities, and it develops trust and a feeling of safety, particularly important because the First Step work requires such total exposure of one's inner secrets. The following are suggestions that this group worked out. Use them as a model only, and develop your own additional guidelines:

1. Only one person at a time speaks, uninterrupted, always.

2. Each speaker takes the floor by stating his or her name: "I'm Ann...." Although it sounds artificial, it makes it clear whose turn it is.

3. He or she has the floor until relinquishing it by saying something like "Thanks" or "That's all."

4. When the other members are sure that the speaker is finished, ask for permission to give feedback.

5. The speaker has the right to refuse or stop feedback at any time, even if he or she has previously approved it—without having to give any explanations.

6. Try to limit feedback to reflecting on what you saw or felt, rather than providing advice or analysis. Avoid intellectualizing about your personal experiences.

7. Compassion is welcome, but remember—our feelings are our feelings. We don't need to be persuaded out of them.

8. If you have a problem with something said during someone else's time, use your own time to discuss it, or wait until after the meeting.

9. Try to avoid sarcasm or other types of aggressive or negative comments during the meeting.

**Gentleness Notes**

When the work gets really deep on the First Step and the Fourth and Fifth Steps, it will be tempting to think of excuses not to go to a meeting. That is when it is most important for the group to be supportive and encouraging. Connecting on the phone during the week in a buddy system helps keep everyone working together.

Build gentleness into your group process. Allow for breaks from the work and rewards for completing each Step.

# Appendix C

# The Wisdom of the Big Books

THERE ARE NOW over forty Twelve Step fellowships that support recovery from a wide range of addictions and compulsions. These fellowships are listed in Appendix E, including contact information for each.

Eighteen of these fellowships have their own textbooks that serve the same function as AA's *Alcoholics Anonymous,* also called the Big Book; three others—Pills Anonymous, Sexual Recovery Anonymous, and Survivors of Incest Anonymous—are in the process of creating their own textbooks as this volume goes to press.

All of these books are grounded solidly in the Twelve Steps and Twelve Traditions, yet each is unique. Each also offers readers *from all fellowships* much that is uniquely valuable.

When we read not only our own fellowship's textbook, but those of other fellowships, we deepen our discernment, develop an ever-wider perspective, and find greater wisdom and sanity. Furthermore, each fellowship—and each of us in recovery—can learn from the evolution, experiences, successes, and mistakes of other fellowships.

Reading and learning from a fellowship's textbook does not mean you need to attend that fellowship's meetings. But we can all learn from what every textbook teaches—and, as you will discover, every fellowship is a treasure in its own way.

Following is a list of the fellowships that have (or soon will have) textbooks, as well as the titles of those books. In some cases, sections, chapters, or topics of special value are noted.

| Fellowship | Textbook | Special Value |
|---|---|---|
| Adult Children Anonymous | ACA Big Red Book | |
| Adult Children of Alcoholics | ACA Fellowship Text | |
| Al-Anon/Alateen | Al-Anon's Twelve Steps & Twelve Traditions | The erosion of spiritual life |
| Alcoholics Anonymous | Alcoholics Anonymous | |
| Anorexics and Bulimics Anonymous | Anorexics and Bulimics Anonymous | |
| Co-Dependents Anonymous | Codependents Anonymous | Grief |
| Debtors Anonymous | A Currency of Hope | The concept of vagueness |
| Eating Addictions Anonymous | EDA Step Workbook | |
| Emotions Anonymous | Emotions Anonymous | |
| Gamblers Anonymous | Sharing Recovery Through GA | |
| Narcotics Anonymous | Narcotics Anonymous | How the spirit of the Twelve Steps can be manifested in an organization |
| Nicotine Anonymous | Nicotine Anonymous | |
| Pills Anonymous | Title to be determined | Now being written |

| Fellowship | Textbook | Special Value |
|---|---|---|
| Recovering Couples Anonymous | *Recovering Couples Anonymous* | |
| Self-Sabotagers Anonymous | *When Misery Is Company* | |
| Sex Addicts Anonymous | *Sex Addicts Anonymous/Green Book* | How the spirit of the Twelve Steps can be manifested in an organization |
| Sex and Love Addicts Anonymous | *Sex and Love Addicts Anonymous* | |
| Sexaholics Anonymous | *Sexaholics Anonymous* | |
| Sexual Compulsives Anonymous | *Sexual Compulsives Anonymous/The Blue Book* | |
| Sexual Recovery Anonymous | To be determined | Now being written |
| Survivors of Incest Anonymous | To be determined | Now being written |
| Workaholics Anonymous | *WA Book of Recovery* | |

# Appendix D

# Suggested Readings

Alcoholics Anonymous World Services, Inc. *Alcoholics Anonymous,* 4th ed. New York: Alcoholics Anonymous World Services, 2001.

Alcoholics Anonymous World Services, Inc. *Twelve Steps and Twelve Traditions.* New York, Alcoholics Anonymous World Services, 1981.

Amen, Daniel G. *Making a Good Brain Great.* New York: Three Rivers Press, 2006.

Anderson, Louie. *Dear Dad: Letters from an Adult Child.* New York: Penguin, 1991.

Andrews, Andy. *The Noticer.* Nashville, TN: Thomas Nelson, 2009.

Anonymous. *Hope & Recovery: A Twelve Step Guide for Healing from Compulsive Sexual Behavior.* Center City, MN: Hazelden, 1994.

B., Bill. *Compulsive Overeater.* Center City, MN: Hazelden, 1988.

Baars, Conrad. *Born Only Once: The Miracle of Affirmation.* Quincy, IL: Franciscan Herald Press, 2001.

Beattie, Melody. *Beyond Codependency: And Getting Better All the Time.* Center City, MN: Hazelden, 1989.

Becker, Ernest. *The Denial of Death.* New York: The Free Press, 1997.

Black, Claudia. *Double Duty: Help for the Adult Child.* New York: Ballantine, 1990.

Bradshaw, John. *Bradshaw On: The Family: A New Way of Creating Solid Self-Esteem,* revised ed. Deerfield Beach, FL: Health Communications, Inc., 1990.

Bradshaw, John. *Creating Love: The Next Great Stage of Growth.* New York: Bantam, 1994.

Bradshaw, John. *Healing the Shame That Binds You,* revised ed. Deerfield Beach, FL: Health Communications, 2005.

Campbell, Joseph. *The Hero with a Thousand Faces,* 3rd ed. Novato, CA: New World Library, 2008.

Carnes, Patrick. *Don't Call It Love: Recovery from Sexual Addiction.* New York: Bantam, 1992.

Carnes, Patrick. *Facing the Shadow: Starting Sexual and Relationship Recovery,* 2nd ed. Carefree, AZ: Gentle Path Press, 2006.

Carnes, Patrick. *Out of the Shadows: Understanding Sexual Addiction,* 3rd ed. Center City, MN: Hazelden, 2001.

Carnes, Patrick. *Recovery Zone, Volume 1: Making Changes That Last: The Internal Tasks.* Carefree, AZ: Gentle Path Press, 2009.

Carnes, Patrick. *Sexual Anorexia: Overcoming Sexual Self-Hatred.* Center City, MN: Hazelden, 1997.

Carnes, Patrick, Debra Laaser, and Mark Laaser. *Open Hearts: Renewing Relationships with Recovery, Romance, and Reality.* Carefree, AZ: Gentle Path Press, 1999.

Carnes, Patrick, Stefanie Carnes, and John Bailey. *Facing Addiction: Starting Recovery from Alcohol and Drugs.* Carefree, AZ: Gentle Path Press, 2011.

Chodron, Pema. *Comfortable with Uncertainty: 108 Teachings on Cultivating Fearlessness and Compassion.* Boston: Shambhala, 2003.

Chodron, Pema. *The Places That Scare You: A Guide to Fearlessness in Difficult Times.* Boston: Shambhala, 2005.

Chodron, Pema. *Taking the Leap: Freeing Ourselves from Old Habits and Fears.* Boston: Shambhala, 2010.

Chodron, Pema. *When Things Fall Apart: Heart Advice for Difficult Times.* Boston: Shambhala, 2002.

Covey, Stephen R. *The Seven Habits of Highly Effective People,* revised ed. New York: Free Press, 2004.

Covington, Stephanie, and Liana Beckett. *Leaving the Enchanted Forest: The Path from Relationship Addiction to Intimacy.* San Francisco: HarperOne, 1988.

Csikszentmihalyi, Mihaly. *Flow: The Psychology of Optimal Experience.* New York: HarperCollins, 2008.

Earle, Ralph, and Gregory Crow. *Lonely All the Time: Recognizing, Understanding, and Overcoming Sex Addiction, for Addicts and Co-Dependents*. New York: HarperCollins, 1998.

Feinstein, David, and Peg Elliott Mayo. *Rituals for Living and Dying: How We Can Turn Loss and the Fear of Death into an Affirmation of Life*. San Francisco: HarperOne, 1990.

Fossum, Merle A., and Marilyn J. Mason. *Facing Shame: Families in Recovery*. New York: W.W. Norton & Company, 1989.

Frankl, Viktor. *Man's Search for Meaning*. Boston: Beacon Press, 2006.

Geller, Anne. *Restore Your Life: A Living Plan for Sober People*. New York: Bantam Books, 1992.

Geringer Woititz, Janet. *Adult Children of Alcoholics*, expanded ed. Deerfield Beach, FL: Health Communications, 1990.

Goleman, Daniel. *The Brain and Emotional Intelligence: New Insights*. Northampton, MA: More Than Sound, 2011.

Goleman, Daniel. *Emotional Intelligence*. New York: Bloomsbury, 2010.

Goleman, Daniel. *The Meditative Mind: The Varieties of Meditative Experience*. New York: Tarcher, 1996.

Goleman, Daniel. *Social Intelligence: The New Science of Human Relationships*. New York: Bantam, 2007.

Gunaratana, Bhante. *Meditation in Plain English*. Boston: Wisdom Publications, 2011.

Hagen, Steve. *Meditation Now or Never*. San Francisco: HarperOne, 2007.

Hanh, Thich Nhat. *The Miracle of Mindfulness: An Introduction to the Practice of Meditation*. Boston: Beacon Press, 1999.

Hirschfield, Jerry. *The Twelve Steps for Everyone...Who Really Wants Them*, revised ed. Center City, MN: Hazelden, 1987.

Kabat-Zinn, Jon. *Coming to Our Senses: Healing Ourselves and the World Through Mindfulness*. New York: Hyperion, 2006.

Kabat-Zinn, Jon. *Wherever You Go, There You Are*. New York: Hyperion, 2005.

Klausner, Mary Ann, and Bobbie Hasselbring. *Aching for Love: The Sexual Drama of the Adult Child*. San Francisco: HarperOne, 1990.

Kurtz, Ernest and Katherine Ketcham. *The Spirituality of Imperfection: Storytelling and the Search for Meaning.* New York: Bantam, 1993.

Larsen, Earnie. *Stage II Relationships: Love Beyond Addiction.* San Francisco: HarperOne, 1987.

Levine, Stephen. *Unattended Sorrow.* Emmaus, PA: Rodale, 2006.

May, Gerald. *Addiction and Grace: Love and Spirituality in the Healing of Addictions.* San Francisco: HarperOne, 2007.

Millman, Dan. *Way of the Peaceful Warrior,* Revised ed. Tiburon, CA: H.J. Kramer, 2006.

Nouwen, Henri J.M. *Reaching Out: The Three Movements of the Spiritual Life.* New York: Image, 1986.

Peck, M. Scott. *The Road Less Traveled, 25th Anniversary Edition.* New York: Touchstone, 2003.

St. John of the Cross (Mirabai Starr, translator). *Dark Night of the Soul.* New York: Riverhead, 2003.

Schneider, Jennifer P. *Back from Betrayal: Recovering from His Affairs,* 3rd ed. Tucson, AZ: Recovery Resources Press, 2005.

Sheperd, Scott. *Survival Handbook: For the Newly Recovering.* Minneapolis, MN: CompCare, 1988.

Siegel, Daniel J. *Mindsight: The New Science of Personal Transformation.* New York: Bantam, 2010.

Tillich, Paul. *The Courage to Be.* New Haven, CT: Yale University Press, 2000.

# Appendix E

# Twelve Step Support Group Information

**Adult Children Anonymous/Adult Children of Alcoholics**
**adultchildren.org**
> Box 3216
> Torrance, CA 90510
> 562-595-7831

**Al-Anon**
**al-anon.org**
> 1600 Corporate Landing Parkway
> Virginia Beach, VA 23454
> 757-563-1600
> Fax: 757-563-1655
> E-mail: wso@al-anon.org

**Alateen**
**al-anon.alateen.org**
> 1600 Corporate Landing Parkway
> Virginia Beach, VA 23454
> 757-563-1600
> Fax: 757-563-1655
> E-mail: wso@al-anon.org

**Alcoholics Anonymous**
**aa.org**
> Box 459
> New York, NY 10163
> 212-870-3400

**Anorexics and Bulimics Anonymous**
**aba12steps.org**
Box 125
Edmonton, AB T5J 2G9 Canada
780.318.6355
E-mail: aba@shawbiz.ca

**Chapter 9—Couples in Recovery Anonymous**
**chapter9-nyc.org**
Box 245
New York, NY 10159
212-946-1874; 888-799-6463 (toll free)
E-mail: info@chapter9couplesinrecovery.org

**Cocaine Anonymous**
**ca.org**
Box 492000
Los Angeles, CA 90049-8000
*also*
21720 S. Wilmington Ave., Suite 304
Long Beach, CA 90810-1641
310-559-5833
Fax: 310-559-2554
E-mail: cawso@ca.org

**Co-Anon and Co-Ateen** (for relatives and friends of cocaine addicts)
**Co-anon.org**
Box 12722
Tucson, AZ 85732-2722
520-513-5028; 800-898-9985 (toll free)
E-mail: info@co-anon.org

**COSA** (for coaddicts whose lives have been affected by other people's compulsive sexual behavior)
**cosa-recovery.org**
Box 79908
Houston, TX 77279-9908
866-899-2672
E-mail: info@cosa-recovery.org

**Co-Dependents Anonymous (CoDA)**
**coda.org**
>Box 33577
>Phoenix, AZ 85067-3577
>602-277-7991; 888-444-2359 (toll free, English);
>888-444-2379 (toll free, Spanish)
>E-mail: outreach@coda.org

**Compulsive Eaters Anonymous/HOW**
**ceahow.org**
>5500 East Atherton St., Suite 227-B
>Long Beach, CA 90815-4017
>562-342-9344
>Fax: 562-342-9345
>E-mail: gso@ceahow.org

**Crystal Meth Anonymous**
**crystalmeth.org**
>4470 W. Sunset Blvd, Suite 107, Box 555
>Los Angeles, CA 90027-6302
>213-488-4455

**Debtors Anonymous**
**debtorsanonymous.org**
>Box 920888
>Needham, MA 02492-0009
>781-453-2743; 800-421-2383 (toll free)
>Fax: 781-453-2745
>E-mail: office@debtorsanonymous.org

**Double Trouble in Recovery**
(for people with addictions and mental illnesses)
**scshare.com/downloads/DTR_Brochure.pdf** (downloadable brochure)
**youtube.com/watch?v=Akma7v9Ik_A**
(Hazelden "Double Trouble in Recovery" video)
803-727-4631

**Dual Recovery Anonymous**
(for people with addictions and mental illnesses)
**draonline.org**
> Box 8107
> Prairie Village, KS 66208
> 913-991-2703
> E-mail: draws@draonline.org

**Eating Addictions Anonymous**
**eatingaddictionsanonymous.org**
> Box 8151
> Silver Spring, MD 20907-8151
> 202-882-6528
> E-mail: eaagso@eatingaddictionsanonymous.org

**Eating Disorders Anonymous**
**eatingdisordersanonymous.org**
> Box 55876
> Phoenix, AZ 85078-5876
> E-mail: info@eatingdisordersanonymous.org

**Emotions Anonymous**
(for people working toward recovery from emotional difficulties)
**emotionsanonymous.org**
> Box 4245
> St. Paul, MN 55104-0245
> 651-647-9712
> Fax: 651-647-1593

**Families Anonymous**
(for anyone in recovery from the effects of a loved one's addiction)
**familiesanonymous.org**
> 701 Lee Street, Suite 670
> Des Plaines, IL 60016-4508
> Phone: 847-294-5877; 800-736-9805 (toll free)
> Fax: 847-294-5837

**Food Addicts in Recovery Anonymous**
**foodaddicts.org**
>400 W. Cummings Park, Suite 1700
>Woburn, MA 01801
>781-932-6300
>E-mail: office@foodaddicts.org

**Gamblers Anonymous**
**gamblersanonymous.org**
>Box 17173
>Los Angeles, CA 90017
>626-960-3500 (office); 888-424-3577 (helpline)
>Fax: 626-960-3501
>E-mail: isomain@gamblersanonymous.org

**Heroin Anonymous**
**heroin-anonymous.org**
>5025 N. Central Avenue, #587
>Phoenix, AZ 85012

**Incest Survivors Anonymous**
**lafn.org/medical/isa/home.html**
>Box 17245
>Long Beach, CA 90807-7245
>562-428-5599

**Marijuana Anonymous**
**marijuana-anonymous.org**
>Box 7807
>Torrance, CA 90504
>800-766-6779
>E-mail: office@marijuana-anonymous.org

**Nar-Anon** (for relatives and friends of people with drug addictions)
**nar-anon.org**
>22527 Crenshaw Blvd., Suite 200B
>Torrance, CA 90505
>310-534-8188; 800-477-6291 (toll free)

**Narcotics Anonymous**
**na.org**
>Box 9999
>Van Nuys, CA 91409
>818-773-9999
>Fax: 818-700-0700

**Nicotine Anonymous**
**nicotine-anonymous.org**
>6333 E. Mockingbird, #147-817
>Dallas, TX 75214
>877-879-6422
>E-mail: info@nicotine-anonymous.org

**Online Gamers Anonymous**
**olganon.org**
>104 Miller Lane
>Harrisburg, PA 17110
>612-245-1115

**Overeaters Anonymous**
**oa.org**
>Box 44020
>Rio Rancho, NM 87174-4020
>505-891-2664
>Fax: 505-891-4320

**Pills Anonymous**
**pillsanonymous.org**

**Recovering Couples Anonymous**
**recovering-couples.org**
>Box 11029
>Oakland, CA 94611
>781-794-1456; 877-663-2317 (toll free)

**S-Anon and S-Ateen**
(for people who have been affected by others' sexual behavior)
**sanon.org**
>   Box 111242
>   Nashville, TN 37222-1242
>   615-833-3152; 800-210-8141 (toll free)
>   E-mail: sanon@sanon.org

**Self Sabotagers Anonymous/Misery Addicts Anonymous**
**miseryaddicts.org**

**Sex Addicts Anonymous**
**sexaa.org**
>   Box 70949
>   Houston, TX 77270
>   713-869-4902; 800-477-8191 (toll free)
>   E-mail: info@saa-recovery.org

**Sex and Love Addicts Anonymous**
**slaafws.org**

**Sexaholics Anonymous**
**sa.org**
>   Box 3565
>   Brentwood, TN 37024
>   615-370-6062; 866-424-8777 (toll free)
>   Fax: 615-370-0882
>   E-mail: saico@sa.org

**Sexual Compulsives Anonymous**
**sca-recovery.org**
>   Box 1585, Old Chelsea Station
>   New York, NY 10011
>   212-606-3778; 800-977-4325 (toll free)

**Sexual Recovery Anonymous**
**sexualrecovery.org**
>   Box 178
>   New York, NY 10276
>   E-mail: info@sexualrecovery.org

**Spenders Anonymous**
**spenders.org**

**Survivors of Incest Anonymous**
**siawso.org**
    Box 190
    Benson, MD 21018-9998
    410-893-3322

**Workaholics Anonymous**
**workaholics-anonymous.org**
    Box 289
    Menlo Park, CA 94026-0289
    510-273-9253
    E-mail: wso@workaholics-anonymous.org

**www.12step.org**
(for anyone dealing with any addictive or dysfunctional behavior)

# Appendix F

# Recovery Resources from Dr. Patrick Carnes and Associates

*Gentle Path Press* provides a wide range of recovery resources, including books, workbooks, audios, videos, posters, and the *Recovery Start Kit*, which provides guidance, support, and inspiration for the first 130 days of recovery. Many of these resources are written or cowritten by Patrick Carnes. The Gentle Path site also offers FAQs on sexual addiction and sexual anorexia, links to recovery fellowships, and a tool to help locate a therapist.

> **gentlepath.com**
> Box 3172
> Carefree, AZ 85377
> Toll Free: 800-708-1796
> Office: 480-488-0150; 800-708-1796 (toll free)
> E-mail: info@gentlepath.com

*International Institute for Trauma and Addiction Professionals* (IITAP) promotes professional training and knowledge of sexual addiction and related disorders. Sex addiction affects the lives of millions of people worldwide, and practicing therapists are on the front lines, treating this epidemic. IITAP offers three certifications to addiction treatment professionals: Certified Sex Addiction Therapist (CSAT), Certified Multiple Addiction Therapist (CMAT), and Associate Sex Addiction Therapist (ASAT). Its website, iitap.com, is the leading online resource for sex addiction professionals. It includes a wide range of useful resources for mental health professionals, including articles, newsletters, links, upcoming events and trainings, an online forum, and an online tool for locating a sex addiction therapist.

**iitap.com**
Box 2112
Carefree, AZ 85377
480-575-6853; 866-575-6853 (toll free)
Fax: 480-595-4753
E-mail: info@iitap.com

*Patrickcarnes.com* provides detailed information on upcoming talks, presentations, workshops, and other events featuring Patrick Carnes and his colleagues.

*Recoveryzone.com* offers a regular newsletter on recovery, plus several free anonymous assessments: a sexual addiction screening test, a sexual addiction risk assessment, and a partner sexuality survey.

*Sexhelp.com* offers a wealth of free resources, information, and inspiration for sex addicts and people in recovery from sexual addiction. The site includes on-line tests, articles, FAQs, and news of upcoming events, plus links to Twelve Step fellowships, recovery centers, and other helpful organizations.

*Sexhelpworkshops.com* provides details on many upcoming workshops, programs, and trainings offered by Patrick Carnes and his colleagues.

*Sexualaddictiontherapists.com* offers a variety of articles and videos on sexual addiction, a free sexual addiction screening test, and links to helpful resources of all types.

# Notes

1. Jacobs-Stewart, T. (2010). *Mindfulness and the 12 Steps: Living Recovery in the Present Moment.* Center City, MN: Hazelden.

2. Schuckit, M.A., Goodwin, D.A., and Winokur, G. (1972). "A Study of Alcoholism in Half Siblings." *American Journal of Psychiatry* 128: 1132–1136.

3. Amen, D. G. (1999). *Change Your Brain, Change Your Life: The Breakthrough Program for Conquering Anxiety, Depression, Obsessiveness, Anger, and Impulsiveness.* New York: Three Rivers Press.

4. Pitchers, K. K., Balfour, M. E., Lehman, M. N., Richtand, N. M., Yu, L., and Coolen, L. M. (2010). "Neuroplasticity in the Mesolimbic System Induced by Natural Reward and Subsequent Reward Abstinence." *Biological Psychiatry* 67, 872–879. Also see Hilton, D. L. and Watts, C. (2011). "Pornography Addiction: A Neuroscience Perspective." *Surgical Neurology International* 2:1.

5. Cozolino, Louis (2002). *The Neuroscience of Psychotherapy: Building and Rebuilding the Human Brain.* New York: Norton.

6. Ibid.

7. Spada, M. M. and Wells, A. (2009). A metacognitive model of problem drinking. *Clinical Psychology and Psychotherapy* 16, 383–393.

8. Siegel, D.J. (2006). "An Interpersonal Neurobiology Approach to Psychotherapy: Awareness, Mirror Neurons, and Neural Plasticity in the Development of Well-Being." *Psychiatric Annals* 36:4.

9. Siegel, D. J. (2007). *The Mindful Brain: Reflection and Attunement in the Cultivation of Well-Being.* New York: Norton, p. 160.

10. Amen, D. G. (1999). *Change Your Brain, Change Your Life.*

11. Ibid.

12. Siegel, "An Interpersonal Neurobiology Approach."

13. Redish, A. D., Jensen, S., and Johnson, A. (2008). "A Unified Framework for Addiction: Vulnerabilities in the Decision Process." *Behavioral and Brain Sciences* 31, 415–487.

14. Frankl, V. (1959). *Man's Search for Meaning.* Boston: Beacon Press, 176.

# About the Author

**Patrick J. Carnes, Ph.D.,** is an internationally known authority on addiction and recovery issues. He has authored over twenty books including the bestselling titles *Out of the Shadows: Understanding Addiction Recovery, Betrayal Bond, Don't Call It Love,* and the first edition of *A Gentle Path Through the Twelve Steps.* Dr. Carnes's research provides the architecture for the "task model" of treating addictions that is used by thousands of therapists worldwide and many well-known treatment centers, residential facilities, and hospitals. He is the executive director of the Gentle Path Program at Pine Grove Behavioral Health in Hattiesburg, Mississippi, which specializes in dedicated treatment for sexual addiction. For more information on his work and contributions, log on to patrickcarnes.com and sexhelp.com. You can also find him on Facebook and Twitter.

## About Hazelden Publishing

As part of the Hazelden Betty Ford Foundation, Hazelden Publishing offers both cutting-edge educational resources and inspirational books. Our print and digital works help guide individuals in treatment and recovery, and their loved ones. Professionals who work to prevent and treat addiction also turn to Hazelden Publishing for evidence-based curricula, digital content solutions, and videos for use in schools, treatment programs, correctional programs, and electronic health records systems. We also offer training for implementation of our curricula.

Through published and digital works, Hazelden Publishing extends the reach of healing and hope to individuals, families, and communities affected by addiction and related issues.

For more information about Hazelden publications,
please call **800-328-9000**
or visit us online at **hazelden.org/bookstore.**

Excerpt from

# *A Gentle Path through the Twelve Principles*

by Patrick Carnes, Ph.D.

PRINCIPLES REPRESENT a higher level of learning and thinking than rules or guidelines do. A rule is something to follow, usually in the precise way prescribed, but a principle is something to reflect on, implement, and live into.

Like recipes, the Twelve Principles allow for some variation and modification. You can follow a recipe for pancakes to the letter, or you can add more blueberries (or more flour or more eggs) to create something slightly different but delicious and nourishing nonetheless. Still, there are limits: replace the blueberries with codfish and your pancakes become unmanageable. Furthermore, sometimes recipes *need* to be modified. If you're baking bread at 8,000 feet, you need to alter the recipe to get the same results you would at sea level.

We folks in recovery often have difficulty managing our feelings. We hate the discomfort of being upset or afraid or angry. We also typically try to avoid uncertainty, which can cause us great anxiety. Unfortunately, one way many of us deal with anxiety and uncertainty is by turning flexible principles into rigid rules. We make them sacred or even sacramental—thus creating needless trouble for ourselves and others. If you catch yourself doing this with the Twelve Principles, remind yourself that this is one more form of stinking thinking, and talk with your sponsor or someone else you trust in the program. Also remind yourself that the Principles offer us the most benefit, and the most hope, when we let them live inside us as healthy, adaptable organisms.

Unlike the Twelve Steps or the Serenity Prayer, the Twelve Principles are not a set of texts to be memorized or recited. Rather, they are a paradigm: a way of viewing and being in the world. Putting the Principles into practice in our lives shifts our internal paradigm: the rules, beliefs, and processes through which we perceive things go through a fundamental change.

Although this book is built around the Twelve Principles, it is not limited to them.

We'll begin with a look at the neuroscience behind the Principles. We now know, for example, that the basic neurology of recovery involves literally regrowing our brains, creating new and healthier ways of thinking, perceiving, and acting which can eventually actually build new neural pathways that sustain those behaviors and thought patterns. Next we'll dig into the Twelve Principles, devoting a chapter to each, and look at how each one relates to the relevant Step. We'll also ask the essential question embedded in each Principle. Here are the Steps, each with its correlative Principle and key question.

| Step | Principle | Key Question |
|---|---|---|
| 1. We admitted we were powerless over alcohol—that our lives had become unmanageable. | Acceptance | What are my limits? |
| 2. Came to believe that a Power greater than ourselves could restore us to sanity. | Awareness | How do I know what is real? |
| 3. Made a decision to turn our will and our lives over to the care of God *as we understood Him.* | Spirituality | Am I lovable to God and others? |
| 4. Made a searching and fearless moral inventory of ourselves. | Responsibility | Who am I? |
| 5. Admitted to God, to ourselves, and to another human being the exact nature of our wrongs. | Openness | How do I trust? |

| | | |
|---|---|---|
| 6. Were entirely ready to have God remove all these defects of character. | Honesty | What must improve? |
| 7. Humbly asked Him to remove our shortcomings. | Courage | What risks must I take? |
| 8. Made a list of all the persons we had harmed, and became willing to make amends to them all. | Commitment | How am I responsible? |
| 9. Made direct amends to such people whenever possible, except when to do so would injure them or others. | Responsiveness | What is integrity? |
| 10. Continued to take personal inventory and when we were wrong promptly admitted it. | Trust Process | How do I live not knowing outcomes? |
| 11. Sought through prayer and meditation to improve our conscious contact with God *as we understood Him,* praying only for knowledge of His will for us and the power to carry that out. | Meaning | What is the purpose of my life? |
| 12. Having had a spiritual awakening as the result of these steps, we tried to carry this message to alcoholics, and to practice these principles in all our affairs. | Generativity | How do I pass it on? |

In the first few chapters of this book we look at five key elements of our lives—sex, money, work, intimacy, and lifestyle—in relation to each of the Principles. In the final chapters we examine the wisdom of the Principles as found in the various fellowships' textbooks (such as *Alcoholics Anonymous, Narcotics Anonymous,* and *Sex and Love Addicts Anonymous*). We also consider how to solve everyday problems using the Twelve Principles, and we discuss how to hold a group meeting based on the Principles.